EXPENDITURES OF OLDER AMERICANS

Expenditures of Older Americans

ROSE M. RUBIN
and
MICHAEL L. NIESWIADOMY

Westport, Connecticut
London

Library of Congress Cataloging-in-Publication Data

Rubin, Rose M.
    Expenditures of older Americans / by Rose M. Rubin and Michael L.
Nieswiadomy.
      p. cm.
    Includes bibliographical references and indexes.
    ISBN 0–275–95874–4 (alk. paper)
    1. Aged—United States—Finance, Personal. 2. Retirement income—
United States. 3. Aged—United States—Economic conditions.
I. Nieswiadomy, Michael. II. Title.
HG179.R76   1997
332.024'0565—dc21   97–19755

British Library Cataloguing in Publication Data is available.

Library of Congress Catalog Card Number: 97–19755
ISBN: 0–275–95874–4

First published in 1997

Praeger Publishers, 88 Post Road West, Westport, CT 06881
An imprint of Greenwood Publishing Group, Inc.

Printed in the United States of America

The paper used in this book complies with the
Permanent Paper Standard issued by the National
Information Standards Organization (Z39.48–1984).

10 9 8 7 6 5 4 3 2 1

Copyright Acknowledgments

The author and publisher gratefully acknowledge permission for use of the following material:

Excerpts from Rose M. Rubin and Michael Nieswiadomy, "Economic Adjustments of Households on Entry into Retirement," *Journal of Applied Gerontology* 14, no. 4, pp. 467–482, copyright © 1995 by Sage Publications, Inc. Reprinted by permission of Sage Publications, Inc.

Excerpts from Rose M. Rubin and Kenneth Koelln, "Determinants of Out-of-Pocket Health Expenditures," copyright © 1993 in *Social Science Quarterly*; by permission of the University of Texas Press.

Excerpts from Rose M. Rubin, Kenneth Koelln, and Roger Speas, "The Impact of Medigap Insurance on Out-of-Pocket Health Expenditures by Older Americans over the 1980s," *Journal of Economics and Finance* 19, no. 2, 1995, pp. 153–170. Reprinted by permission of the *Journal of Economics and Finance*.

Excerpts from Michael Nieswiadomy and Rose M. Rubin, "Changes in Expenditure Patterns of Retirees: 1972–1973 and 1986–1987," *Journal of Gerontology: Social Sciences* 50B, no. 5, 1995, pp. S274–S290. Reprinted by permission of the Gerontological Society of America.

For Dick, Mark and Alyson, Debra and Chris
For Claire, Ben, Daniel, and David

Contents

Figures and Tables

Preface

Issues of the economics of aging have been of special interest to the authors of this book for some years, combining concerns for the social and economic welfare of individuals and families with numerous current public policy issues that will have increasing budgetary impacts. This text provides substantive contributions that will materially inform researchers, students, decision makers, service providers, and others concerned about aging in the United States.

The authors' empirical research reported in this book was supported by a series of three competitive grants received from the AARP Andrus Foundation between 1990 and 1994. We are thankful for their substantial support, without which this research could not have been accomplished. The principal investigator on each of these projects was Dr. Rose M. Rubin, who developed and maintained the concept for this book as an underlying theme motivating the proposals for these grants. Dr. Michael Nieswiadomy and Dr. Bobye J. Riney were co-investigators on the first AARP grant, and Dr. Kenneth Koelln was a co-investigator on the other two AARP projects. Additional support was received from University of North Texas Faculty Research Grants and the Texas Institute for Research and Education on Aging.

The completely original material in this book consists of Chapters 1, 2, and 7. In addition, while some of the data analysis is original, the major studies reported in Chapters 3 through 6 are based on a series of research articles published by the authors in refereed economics, social sciences, and gerontology journals. Some of these articles were written in conjunction with other researchers, most notably Dr. Kenneth Koelln, associate professor in the Department of Economics at the University of North Texas, who found it necessary to decline coauthorship on this book due to other commitments.

Other researchers also contributed to the research reported, including: Dr. Bobye J. Riney, professor emeritus of the University of North Texas; Dr. Marion Smith Picard, research economist at BlueCross\BlueShield of Texas; and Roger Speas of the SAS Institute. The technical assistance of several graduate research assistants, Tarique Md Hossain, Charles Wang, Udomrat Katedamrongchai, Roger Speas, and Salina Xu, contributed to the research accomplishments and enhanced their education in applied economic analysis. Their help with data analysis, literature search, and the preparation of graphic materials is appreciated.

We are grateful to the *Social Science Quarterly*, the *Journals of Gerontology: Social Sciences, The Gerontologist, The Journal of Applied Gerontology*, and the *Journal of Economics and Finance* for granting copyright permission for the inclusion of selected published material and tables. Other material was published in the *Monthly Labor Review*, which requires no copyright permission as a U.S. government publication.

We also appreciate the valuable suggestions and critiques of several colleagues who read the manuscript at various stages. Dr. Carolyn Shaw Bell, professor emeritus of Wellesley College, provided detailed feedback and helpful suggestions.

Without the contributions of each of those named, completion of the book would have been difficult. We, of course, take full responsibility for the contents. Additionally, we thank our families for their support and encouragement.

Chapter 1

Introduction

The aging of the population, the increasing proportion of the elderly in the population, and a lengthening active life span are among the more compelling societal changes of the twentieth century, and these trends will be even more pronounced in the twenty-first century. In the United States in 1996, there were nearly 34 million persons age 65 and over, almost 13 percent of the population, with the age cohort 85 and over increasing the most rapidly. Projections indicate that by 2030, there will be over 69 million older Americans, who will constitute 20 percent of the population (U.S. Bureau of the Census, 1997). The rapidly growing elderly population presents challenges to families and policymakers to provide financial and other support, health care, and special services. This crucial demographic shift also provides opportunities for those businesses that recognize the potential market force of a growing population group with substantial home ownership,[1] relatively little mortgage debt,[2] discretionary income, and the time and inclination for leisure.

Historically, Americans did not live long after retirement. When Social Security was initiated in 1936, over half of the working population did not reach age 65, and very few lived until their late sixties (U.S. Bureau of the Census, 1981). In 1940, the probability that a 65-year-old person would live to age 90 was only 7 percent. By 1992, that probability had more than tripled to 25 percent (U.S. Bureau of the Census, 1996c). Not only are the sheer numbers of older Americans growing, but even more significant is the greater number of retirement years to be planned and financed. The average retirement age has steadily declined toward age 62, since Social Security introduced reduced-benefit provisions for early retirement.[3] By 1990, 65 percent of men and 73 percent of women worker beneficiaries were receiving reduced early retirement benefits, compared to 5 percent of men and 8 percent of women before 1970 (Schulz, 1995). The increase in the older population and their retirement period make their expenditure and consumption patterns significant for both household budgeting and public policy.

Older Americans will live longer, be better educated, and be healthier in the future. Many will be better off financially as a result of dual-earner households, dual pensions, and multiple savings modes. In addition, businesses recognize the potential of older Americans as a target marketing group because of their substantial discretionary income.

Research that acknowledges the heterogeneity of older Americans and identifies distinct group characteristics is needed. The older population is composed of several distinct market groups: the young-old (65–74 years), who are generally active and still married; the old (75–84 years), who are slowing down and often widowed; and the very old (age 85 and older), who often need help in daily activities. The income and expenditures of the young-old and the older age groups are quite different. The young-old benefit from higher Social Security income, as a result of their higher earnings levels, and they have better pensions and asset income.

As the number of elderly persons has increased and the average age of retirement has declined (Moen, 1990; Morris and Bass, 1988), retirees have become a group with substantial power to affect both business and public policy decision making. Businesses and government already respond to the desires and demands of retirees. Examples of government awareness are seen at the national level, where election campaign rhetoric expresses strong consciousness of the voting clout of recipients of Social Security and Medicare, and at the local level, where popular support for school funding is lower in areas with a high percentage of older population.

Business marketing and advertising reflect enhanced awareness of the buying power of older Americans. In our market system, the major perception of a group's wants is through their actual purchases and, over time, through changes in their expenditure patterns. In general, the elderly spend more of their income on housing, food, and health care and less on clothing, transportation, and household furnishings than the nonelderly (Soldo, 1980).

OBJECTIVES OF THE BOOK

Aging in America imposes dramatic personal, social, and economic changes. This book fills the need for an original text and reference source that comprehensively analyzes the economics of older Americans by emphasizing their expenditure patterns, which reflect household lifestyles and quality of life. While many books and articles describe and analyze older Americans, no other text comprehensively treats the expenditures of elderly households.

The text incorporates empirical analyses reporting original research by the authors. The studies reported, as well as the review and synthesis of an extensive literature, provide needed background for researchers and students concerned with issues of aging in America. We present practical information for households for decision making, and we identify and present issues for government policies related to the income and consumption expenditures of older Americans. These analyses highlight the diversity among the household types and the economic situations of older people. They also reveal that clearly targeted policy changes would benefit major subgroups of the elderly.

This research monograph describes the lifestyles of different groups of the elderly through detailed analyses of their expenditure patterns. The broad objective of the book is to present and analyze the expenditure patterns of older households in the United States as indicators of their lifestyles and quality of life. The text fills an important gap in research on older households by presenting the major findings of three research projects funded by the AARP Andrus Foundation.

We concentrate on analyses of the determinants of expenditures for a variety of goods and services by varied groups. Specifically, the book presents: (1) expenditure patterns of elderly households and groups, comparing these over time and with nonelderly households; (2) comparisons of expenditures of retired and nonretired elderly households; (3) detailed analysis of expenditures on necessities (food, housing, health care) by the elderly poor and comparisons with other groups; and (4) detailed analysis of expenditures on health care by the elderly and comparisons with other groups.

CONSUMER EXPENDITURE THEORY

Consumer expenditure theory recognizes that both income and consumption vary over the life cycle. The classical theory of consumption and saving behavior is grounded in two complementary economic theories.

These are the Life Cycle Hypothesis (Ando and Modigliani, 1963) and the Permanent Income Hypothesis (Friedman, 1957), which are widely used to explain household expenditure and saving patterns over time. Both of these approaches indicate that consumer decisions are made on the basis of current and past experiences and future expectations to achieve a relatively consistent lifetime consumption level.

The Life Cycle Hypothesis (Ando and Modigliani, 1963) posits that consumers attempt to maintain a relatively stable consumption level through their lifetime by saving during their maximum earning years and dissaving[4] during retirement. The related Permanent Income Hypothesis (Friedman, 1957) suggests that consumers adjust their spending levels to their perceived level of future income. Thus, the underlying economic theory indicates that rational consumers attempt to ignore the fluctuations of current income around what they perceive to be their permanent income level, and they maximize utility by reducing fluctuations in (or by "smoothing") consumption over time. Both of these theories predict dissaving by retirees.

In an alternate theory, Deaton (1992) suggested that saving behavior reflects differences in tastes. He concluded that elderly persons are extremely cautious about dissaving, due to uncertainty about their life span, future health care costs, and a possible decline into poverty. Thus, he concluded that the permanent income or life cycle effects may be dominated by the precautionary motive for saving among older households.

Frank (1985) proposed another theory based on the notion that people desire positional (i.e., status) goods. A positional good's value depends on its comparison to similar goods consumed by others and thus is inherently scarce. If positional concerns are important, persons in the lower part of the income distribution will struggle to keep up with community consumption standards. This theory predicts that savings will rise with position in the income distribution. Were it not for Social Security and forced retirement savings programs, poor persons would have inadequate retirement incomes. In contrast, the Life Cycle and Permanent Income Hypotheses predict that savings rates are independent of position.

Research on expenditure patterns has generated considerable work on the savings and dissavings of the elderly in retirement. This body of empirical studies does not consistently confirm the life cycle or permanent income theories. Although both of these theories predict dissaving by retirees, numerous empirical studies have found continued saving by the elderly into retirement rather than dissaving (Danziger et al., 1982–83; Mirer, 1979; Stoller and Stoller, 1987; Torrey and Taeuber, 1986; Wilcox, 1991). Other studies found that the elderly dissave at lower rates than the

Life Cycle Hypothesis predicts (Hogarth, 1989; Hurd, 1987, 1989, 1990; Mirer, 1980). Davies (1981) found that the retired elderly dissaved at a rate of 3 to 4 percent per year.

Nearly half of retired households continued to save in retirement (Hogarth, 1989). Danziger and colleagues (1982–83), using 1972–1973 Consumer Expenditure (CE) Survey data and the Inventory of Consumer Durables, found that many elderly households maintain their wealth by reducing consumption. They found that the elderly spent less than the nonelderly at the same level of income and that the very oldest have the lowest average propensities to consume. They concluded that expenditure patterns of older persons were affected by their uncertainty about health, length of life, and the ability to maintain independent households. These findings are consistent with Deaton's (1992) theory of the dominance of the precautionary motive for saving in older households.

Hogarth (1989) reported findings from the Longitudinal Retirement History Survey (LRHS) that focused on characteristics of households who were savers and dissavers during the first eight years of retirement. While nearly half the retired households continued to save and build assets in retirement, she found that 20 percent dissaved at rates they could not sustain over their expected lifetimes. Walker and Schwenk (1991) found that households over age 80 saved but those in their seventies dissaved. Lower income, not poor health or becoming widowed, is the main factor that leads to dissaving (Davies, 1981; Hogarth, 1989).

These studies make clear the need for further research in several areas. Only a few articles, other than the present authors' works, have explicitly compared the expenditure patterns of retired and nonretired elderly, and only one article has so far estimated econometrically the expenditure functions (McConnel and Deljavan, 1983; Schwenk, 1990a; Moehrle, 1990). The studies reported in Chapters 3 through 6 update and expand previous studies of elderly expenditure patterns by disaggregating older households into different demographic or income level groups and by using two-stage and Tobit regression analysis. These analyses provide further empirical tests of the competing theories that seek to describe the expenditure behavior of older households.

DATA: THE CONSUMER EXPENDITURE SURVEY

The data used in the authors' empirical studies are from the Bureau of Labor Statistics (BLS) Consumer Expenditure (CE) Interview Survey tapes. This survey is a national sample of households, representative of the total civilian noninstitutional population.[5] Data collection occurs in 101 areas of the country on an ongoing basis. The interview sample consists of a rotating panel that targets 5,000 consumer units (CUs) or households quarterly for five consecutive quarters, with about 1,250 new CUs cycled into the survey each quarter (Gieseman, 1987).

The data used in our studies are from selected years, with major focus on the 1980s. The specific dates of the data used in each individual study were dictated by its particular research questions. One research objective was to measure change in expenditure patterns over time, with several studies using cross-sectional data for comparison of 1980–1981 with 1989–1990 and one comparative study also using 1972–1973.[6]

The CE Interview Survey tapes contain detailed demographic information and data on expenditure behavior, income, taxes, financial assets, housing ownership, and public assistance for each consumer unit (CU) or household.[7] The broad objective of this survey is to obtain a year of expenditure data from each sample household (Passero, 1996). Data are collected on the types of expenditures that respondents can remember for a period of three months or longer (U.S. Department of Labor, 1992). In general these include relatively large or major expenditures (e.g., real property, automobiles, and major appliances) or expenditures that occur on a fairly regular basis (e.g., rent, utilities, or insurance premiums). These expenditures cover an estimated 60 to 70 percent of total expenditures. An additional 20 to 25 percent is accounted for by "global estimates" of spending for food. Thus, about 95 percent of household expenditures are estimated to be covered in the interview survey (Garner, 1987). Expenditure amounts are recorded as the "transaction costs" (or dollar amounts) for all items purchased, even if the full amount is not paid at the time of purchase, and they include all taxes on the items purchased (Gieseman, 1987).

In the CE Survey, data are also collected on sources and levels of income for individuals and for the household as a unit, for the 12-month period prior to the interview (Passero, 1996). Household income includes cash income from all sources plus the value of food stamps. It does not include other in-kind income such as the value of public housing or Medicare, nor the value derived from durables such as the rental value of owner-occupied housing. In addition, data on both assets and liabilities over the previous year are collected in the fifth interview, so our studies using asset variables either include or consist of the fifth interview.

Each household remaining in the CE Survey for its full survey year is interviewed five times at three-month intervals, with the first interview omitted from the data set. Four quarters of data are reported on each household that remains in the survey for a complete cycle. Although some researchers use each quarter of data as an independent sample, we generally use data aggregated by individual households over several quarters. We do not include households with only one quarter of data because of the large variance of quarterly expenditures, particularly in the medical care category due to the irregular pattern of expenditures on health care. Presenting household expenditures by annual rather than quarterly figures increases accuracy, removes the need for seasonal adjustment, and minimizes possible methodological complications of zeros in the expenditure data, which may occur in the case of health care.[8] The CE Survey data used are those reported by respondents and are not seasonally adjusted. In several studies, the data are pooled for two-year periods to enhance sample size.

The samples studied include only those households that the BLS terms "complete income reporters" with before-tax and after-tax income greater than zero. The BLS defines a complete income reporter as a consumer unit that provides values for at least one of the major sources of its income, such as wages and salaries, self-employment income, and Social Security income. Even complete income reporters may not have provided a full accounting of all income from all sources (U.S. Department of Labor, 1992). Households included in our research are limited to those we define as "living independently," that is, they have total expenditures greater than zero and positive expenditures for both food and housing.

Each study uses a relevant set of screening criteria to select its specific sample population from the CE Survey data. In general, we sampled the age group 50 and over or 65 and over, with additional defined criteria, and we also drew samples of nonelderly households for expenditure comparisons.

ORGANIZATION OF THE BOOK

The book has seven chapters, a preface, an index, and an extensive reference list/bibliography, especially useful to researchers and students. Chapter 1 is an introduction to the book, including its rationale, objectives, and organization. It also describes the U.S. Bureau of Labor Statistics Consumer Expenditure Survey, the database used in the empirical studies. Chapter 2 reviews the demographics and socioeconomic characteristics of the elderly population. The topical areas surveyed include marital status, economic status, income, sources of income, wealth, saving behavior, employment, and labor force participation.

In Chapters 3 through 6, a series of research articles published in diverse gerontology and economics journals by the authors[9] are summarized and synthesized. However, the text remains accessible to a wide variety of readers and scholars interested in issues of aging.

Chapter 3 focuses on changes in retiree expenditures over time. Expenditure shares for three different types of retired and working households (married couple, single male, and single female) are compared by age groups and by income level. Then, econometric models of expenditure functions of retirees in the early 1970s and the mid-1980s are compared.

Chapter 4 examines the economic changes that occur upon entry into retirement and the differing expenditure patterns of retired and nonretired households. The expenditure patterns, income sources, savings, and taxes of retired (age 50+) households are analyzed. We compare changes in consumption patterns of married couples, single males, and single females immediately before and following their retirement, by major expenditure categories and by detailed key categories (health care, leisure activities, and travel).

The vulnerable elderly are the focus of Chapter 5, which discusses poverty demographics and the distribution of income, expenditures on necessities, and the economic vulnerability of older women. We compare expenditures on necessities by those elderly receiving cash assistance (welfare and/or SSI) to those not receiving such income payments and also to those not economically disadvantaged. Impoverished older Americans are less able to sustain their quality of life than higher-income older households. Those in lower-income groups but without AFDC or SSI spent more than their current income and were even more financially distressed than aid recipients. We also analyze changes in expenditures on necessities by elderly and nonelderly households over the decade of the 1980s.

Chapter 6 analyzes out-of-pocket health care and health insurance expenditures by comparing the medical care expenditures of elderly and nonelderly households over time, and by analyzing how Medigap insurance affects health expenditures. Higher- and lower-income elderly exhibit different spending patterns on health care. Lower-income elderly spend a much larger share of their total expenditures on health care, reflecting co-payments and deductibles plus items (such as prescriptions) not covered by Medicare. Contrary to the expectation that insurance coverage lowers out-of-pocket health expenditures, the data show that increased levels of insurance accompany higher levels of health care spending.

Chapter 7 provides a summary and overview of trends in the expenditures and lifestyle changes of older Americans and a perspective on their anticipated lifestyles and economic security into the twenty-first century. We summarize the dominant findings and conclusions derived from our research analyses and relate these to the lifestyles and quality of life of various groups of elderly households. In particular, we focus upon economic security for the elderly and their financial vulnerability, especially that of women. We identify the major current trends among older households highlighted by our study and present likely future scenarios indicated by these trends. The anticipated impacts of the aging population and their lifestyle changes on households and on businesses, as well as on national and state policy formation, are delineated.

NOTES

1. Home ownership clearly increases with age up to age 75. In 1994, compared to 64 percent home ownership for the U.S. population, householders age 50 to 59 had approximately 77 percent home ownership, and over 80 percent of householders age 60 to 75 were home owners, the highest rates for any age category (U.S. Bureau of the Census, 1995, page 736, table 1228).

2. While home ownership increases with age, mortgage and home equity debt decline as the age of the householder increases. In 1992, while 62 percent of those age 45 to 54 held mortgage debt, only 40 percent of those age 55 to 64, 18 percent of those age 65 to 74, and 7 percent of those age 75 and over had mortgage and home equity debt (U.S. Bureau of the Census, 1995, page 517, table 790).

3. Social Security reduced-benefit provisions for early retirement were introduced in 1956 for women and in 1961 for men (Schulz, 1995).

4. Dissaving occurs when current spending exceeds current income.

5. Thus, our studies do not include elderly persons in nursing homes or other institutional settings. Also, in most cases, households including an elderly person who is not the householder are excluded, so elderly households refer to those with the householder age 65 and over.

6. Since the current CE Survey program was begun in 1980, data from the 1972–1973 survey had to be recoded and adapted for comparison with more recent survey data.

7. The BLS defines a consumer unit as a single person living alone or sharing a household with others but who is financially independent; members of a sample household related by blood, marriage, adoption, or other legal arrangement; or two or more persons living together who share responsibility for at least two out of three major types of expenses—food, housing, and other expenses. The terms "household" or "consumer unit" are used interchangeably for convenience (U.S. Department of Labor, 1992). Based on the convention established by the BLS, we use the term "household" throughout the text to designate a consumer unit.

8. In one study, for those households with only two quarters of data, expenditures are doubled to annualize them, and for those with three quarters, expenditure data are multiplied by one and one-third.

9. Several of these articles also had additional coauthors, whose contributions are acknowledged in the preface and can also be seen in the bibliography.

Chapter 2

Characteristics of Older Americans

While the elderly are often considered a single homogenous group, they are actually a very diverse segment of the U.S. population. Simple characterizations or stereotypes of the elderly provide inadequate descriptions. It is generally recognized that elderly households differ from those of the nonelderly both economically and demographically. However, the significant variations among the elderly in terms of income, wealth, family composition, health status, mobility, and quality of life across gender, race, and age categories are less well recognized.

This chapter provides an overview of the past, current, and projected future characteristics of the elderly that impact their incomes and expenditures. Many of these sociodemographic factors are used as explanatory variables in our expenditure models in the following four chapters. Given the heterogeneity of the elderly population, these variables help to explain the significant variations in expenditures on food, clothing, housing, transportation, health care, entertainment, and many other items.

DEMOGRAPHICS AND PROJECTIONS

The demographic characteristics of the elderly population have changed dramatically in the past century. Many of these changes are expected to continue into the next century. In this section we discuss the rapid growth in the elderly population, the lengthening life expectancies, the recent rise in the share of the population over age 85, and the change in the racial diversity of the elderly population.

Growth Rate in the Elderly Population

In this century the growth rate of the elderly population (65 years and older) has greatly exceeded that of the overall population. The elderly population increased more than tenfold, from 3 million in 1900 to nearly 34 million in 1996, in contrast to only a threefold increase in the nonelderly population, from 73 million to 218 million (U.S. Bureau of the Census, 1997). A brief lull in the growth is expected during the 20-year period between 1990 and 2010, as the elderly population expands at a lower rate (1.3 percent per annum) than during any other 20-year period. This reduced growth rate, which derives from the low fertility of the 1930s, will not last long because the baby boomers are approaching retirement.[1] When the baby boomers start turning 65 in 2011, the growth rate will accelerate, causing the elderly population to increase to over 80 million by the middle of the next century. Furthermore, as seen in Table 2.1, their share of the population, which increased from 4 percent in 1900 to 13 percent in 1990, is expected to grow to 20 percent in 2050. At that time the United States will no longer be a nation of the young: there will be more elderly (65 or over) than young (14 or younger) (U.S. Bureau of the Census, 1996c).

Life Expectancies

Another notable occurrence of this century is the lengthening life expectancy of older Americans. In 1900, male life expectancy at age 65 was 11.3 years and female life expectancy was 12.0 years. In 1992 these figures were 15.4 and 18.9, respectively, and it is expected that in 2050 a 65-year-old male's life expectancy will be 17.4 years and a female's will be 22.4 years (see Figure 2.1).[2] The United States is not the only country facing lengthening life expectancies for the elderly. In an international comparison, U.S. life expectancy (at age 65) lies in the middle range of developed countries.[3]

Another perspective on increased longevity is revealed in the percentage of persons age 65 who survive to age 90. Fifty years ago, it was uncommon for someone to live to age 90. In 1940 only 7 percent of 65-year-olds were expected to live to age 90. But by 1992, one-fourth of 65-year-olds were

Table 2.1
Proportion of Population by Age Groups 1900–1996,
with Projections through 2050 (Middle Series)

Year	0-54	55-59	60-64	65+	65-74	75-84	85+
1900	91.0	3.0	2.0	4.0	3.0	1.0	
1910	91.0	3.0	2.0	4.0	3.0	1.0	
1920	90.0	3.0	3.0	4.0	3.0	1.0	
1930	87.0	4.0	3.0	6.0	4.0	2.0	
1940	85.0	4.0	4.0	7.0	5.0	2.0	
1950	83.0	5.0	4.0	8.0	5.0	3.0	
1960	82.0	5.0	4.0	9.0	6.0	3.0	
1970	81.1	4.9	4.2	9.8	6.1	3.0	0.7
1980	79.1	5.1	4.5	11.3	6.9	3.4	1.0
1990	78.9	4.2	4.3	12.6	7.3	4.0	1.3
1996	78.8	4.3	3.8	13.1	7.4	4.3	1.4
2000	78.6	4.8	3.9	12.6	6.6	4.5	1.6
2010	74.6	6.7	5.4	13.2	7.1	4.3	1.9
2020	70.6	6.6	6.4	16.5	9.7	4.8	2.0
2030	69.5	5.1	5.3	20.0	10.8	6.8	2.4
2040	69.5	5.4	4.8	20.3	8.9	7.7	3.7
2050	69.2	5.5	5.2	20.0	8.8	6.6	4.6

Source: U.S. Bureau of the Census, 1994b, *Population projections of the United States by age, sex, race, and hispanic origin: 1995–2050* (Current Population Reports, Series P25–1130).

expected to live to be 90. By the year 2050, the National Center for Health Statistics expects 42 percent to survive to age 90 (U.S. Bureau of the Census, 1996c).

Given the increase in the probability of living many years in retirement, planning retirement expenses has now become a much more complex matter. In the empirical studies described in the following chapters, we examine the significant differences in expenditures for the various age groups of the elderly.[4] The differences in expenditures across the age categories provide further evidence that the elderly are not a homogenous group.

Figure 2.1
Life Expectancies at Age 65: Actual 1900–1990,
Projected 2000–2070

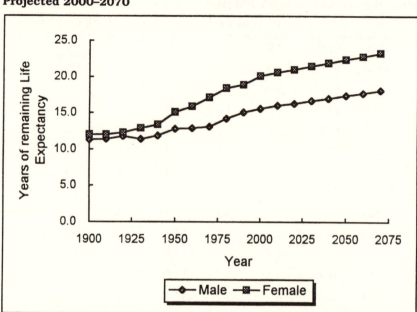

Source: Social Security Administration, 1988, February, *Social Security Bulletin,* 51(2):
       table 14, and U.S. Bureau of the Census, 1995b, *Statistical abstract of the United
       States: 1995,* table 115.

The Oldest Old

The oldest old cohort (age 85+) is the fastest growing segment of the entire population. This age group, which was almost nonexistent in 1900, was
1.2 percent (3 million) of the population by 1990, and is expected to account for 4.6 percent (19 million) by 2050 (U.S. Bureau of the Census,
1996c). Even though this group is still relatively small, it is already large
enough to have a tremendous impact on the nation's health and social service systems (U.S. Council of Economic Advisors, 1997). Further, the oldest old differ markedly from the youngest elderly in their social, economic,
and health characteristics. These differences will become apparent in our
empirical analyses of their spending patterns in Chapters 3–6. In many of
our models we include a dummy variable to capture the effects of this oldest age group on expenditures.

Not only is the oldest old group the fastest growing segment of the population, it is overwhelmingly female. The gender ratio (the number of

males per 100 females) has changed dramatically over a relatively short period of time. In 1930 the gender ratio for the oldest old (85+) was 75, but by 1990 it had declined to only 39. Further, the gender ratio now varies considerably across elderly age groups: 39 for the oldest old compared to 82 for persons 65 to 69 years old. The U.S. Bureau of the Census forecasts that the decline in the gender ratio for the oldest old will partially reverse and will be 60 by 2050 (U.S. Bureau of the Census, 1996c). Even if this partial reversal does occur, women will continue to greatly outnumber men in the age 85+ category.

One consequence of the relative paucity of elderly men is that elderly women are much more likely than elderly men to live alone. In just the past 30 years, the percent of women living alone has doubled. In 1960, 26 percent of women age 75 and over lived alone. By 1994, 52 percent were living alone (see Table 2.2). The combination of men marrying younger women and the greater life expectancy of women contributes to the high number of women living alone. This may not be a problem for some women, with higher incomes that allow them to be independent, but for

Table 2.2
Living Arrangements of the Elderly, Men and Women (Percentage)

	Men				Women			
	With Spouse	Alone	With relatives	With non-relatives	With Spouse	Alone	With relatives	With non-relatives
Age: 65-74								
1960	75	11	10	4	44	23	28	5
1970	76	12	8	4	45	31	20	4
1980	80	11	6	3	48	35	16	1
1990	79	13	6	2	51	34	13	2
1994	78	13	6	3	52	31	15	2
Age: 75+								
1960	57	15	22	6	20	26	46	7
1970	60	20	16	4	21	37	36	6
1980	66	21	11	2	21	48	27	4
1990	66	21	11	2	24	53	20	3
1994	70	21	7	2	26	52	20	2

Note: Noninstitutional population.

Sources: M. D. Hurd, 1990, Research on the elderly: Economic status, retirement, and consumption and saving, *Journal of Economic Literature*, 28(2): 565–637; U.S. Bureau of the Census, 1995, *Statistical abstract of the United States, 1995*, table 62.

many this is distressing because they lack adequate income or assets to maintain financial independence. Due to the importance of this issue, we reserve part of Chapter 5 to analyze the expenditures of poor elderly women.

Diversity

The vast majority of the elderly currently are white, but the racial and ethnic diversity among the elderly is expected to increase in the future. In 1994, only 10 percent (about 3 million) of the elderly was non-white, in comparison to 18 percent for the nonelderly population. Of the elderly, only 2.7 million were black; 137,000 were American Indian, Eskimo, and Aleut; 615,000 were Asian and Pacific Islander; and 1.5 million were Hispanic (who could be of any race).

It is projected that the proportion of elderly who are in a minority group will rise to 20 percent by 2050. Of the 80 million elderly projected for 2050, 8.4 million will be black, 6.7 million will be other than white or black, and 12.5 million will be Hispanic. In 1990, the Hispanic elderly population was less than half the size of the black elderly population but is expected to surpass it in the year 2030 (U.S. Bureau of the Census, 1996c). Our expenditure models described in the following chapters include a race variable to account for the differences in expenditures related to race. These models should provide insight into the effects that changing diversity will have on various expenditure patterns in the future.

WORK AND EDUCATION

The need for consumption planning has become more important in recent decades, not only because of longer life expectancies, but also because of earlier retirement ages. The increase in the number of persons in their early 60s receiving Social Security benefits is one measure indicating a trend toward earlier retirement. In 1974, only 43 percent of insured people aged 62 to 64 received Social Security benefits, but by 1994, 67 percent received benefits. Another measure of earlier retirement is the significant decline in the labor force participation rate of males age 55 to 64 from 83 percent in 1970 to 67 percent in 1996; for males 65 and over the decline was from 27 percent to 17 percent. The change in female labor force participation rates has not been as dramatic. Female participation rates for 55- to 64-year-olds rose from 43 percent to 50 percent, while it declined from 9.7 percent to 8.6 percent for females age 65 and over (see Figure 2.2).

Figure 2.2
Labor Force Participation Rates, 1970–2005:
Males and Females, Age 55–64 and 65+

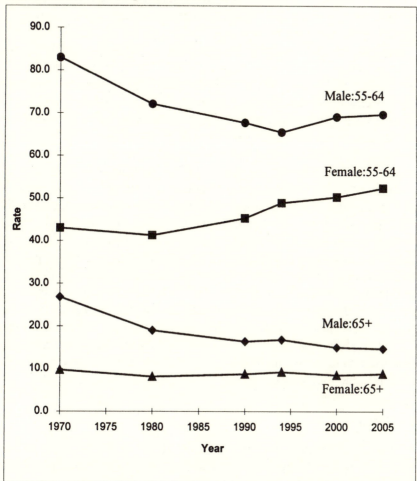

Sources: U.S. Bureau of the Census, 1996c, *65+ in the United States* (Current Population Reports, P23–190).

Labor force participation rates (in 1996) vary inversely with respect to age: from 67 percent for men age 55 to 64, to 28 percent for men age 65 to 69 and 12 percent for men age 70 years and older. Elderly black men have lower labor force participation rates than white men, partly due to health and educational differences (U.S. Bureau of the Census, 1996c).

The work status of the elderly clearly has changed in recent decades. In recognition of the importance of this change in work status, we examine the differences in expenditures of retired and nonretired elderly households in our models in Chapter 4. The differences are quite significant for many of the expenditure categories.

Educational attainment plays a major role in the lives of the elderly, for several reasons. First, research has indicated that more educated persons tend to be healthy longer and economically more prosperous (U.S. Bureau of the Census, 1996c). Secondly, studies have shown that the level of education of the consumer impacts expenditures independent of income levels (Rubin and Nieswiadomy, 1995).

Currently a lower percentage of the elderly (60 percent) have a high school education than persons age 25 to 64 (85 percent). However, the proportion of the elderly with at least a high school education will increase in the ensuing decades because roughly 80 percent of persons age 55 to 59 have at least a high school education. The educational profile of elderly women will change considerably; the share with a bachelor's degree (or higher) is most likely to double in the next forty years. In 1990, 14 percent of elderly men versus 8 percent of elderly women had a bachelor's degree or higher. But by 2030 it is expected that 26 percent of elderly men and 22 percent of elderly women will have at least a bachelor's degree (U.S. Bureau of the Census, 1994a). In order to understand the impact that these changing educational backgrounds of the elderly will have on future consumption patterns, we include an education variable in our expenditure models in the following chapters.

INCOME

One of the greatest concerns, next to health status, that all elderly face is financial security. Many factors impact the attainment of financial security. In this section we discuss the variations in income across time and various sectors of the elderly population, the sources of income, and retirement savings.

Variations in Income

Many of the changes facing the elderly, such as earlier retirement, longer life expectancy, and dependency, are causes for concern. However, elderly household income has improved greatly since 1967, rising 60 percent in real (inflation-adjusted) dollars by 1994. The ratio of income of elderly households to income of all households increased from 0.38 to 0.56 (see

Table 2.3
Median Income and Sources of Income for the Elderly (65+)
(1994 Dollars)

	1967	1976	1984	1986	1994
Median household income					
All households	$29,317	$31,651	$31,972	$33,665	$32,264
65 and over	$11,268	$14,875	$18,256	$18,721	$18,095
Ratio of income of elderly to	0.38	0.47	0.57	0.56	0.56
all households					
Shares of elderly income from:					
Earnings	29	23	16	17	18
Social Security	34	39	38	38	42
Pensions & other retirement	15	16	15	16	19
Assets	15	18	28	26	18
Public assistance	4	2	1	1	1
Other	3	2	2	2	3
Total	100	100	100	100	100

Sources: U.S. Dept. of Health and Human Services, 1996, June, *Income of the population 55 and over 1994*, Social Security Administration, and earlier issues; U.S. Bureau of the Census, 1995a, *Money income in the U.S., 1994* (Current Population Reports, Series P–160–185).

Table 2.3). Although the data are not adjusted for household size or expenses, they do give an indication of the relative economic improvement of the elderly.

Thirty years ago the elderly were perceived as "poor," while today the perception is that the elderly are much better off than other Americans. This view, although partially correct, is overly simplistic. The poverty rate in 1970 was 25 percent for the elderly (over 65) versus 9 percent for persons 18 to 64 years. In 1995, the poverty rate was 10.5 percent for the elderly versus 13.8 percent for the overall population. Thus, while the elderly poverty rate has declined substantially, they are only slightly better off than the overall population. Elderly poverty rates reflect their diversity, varying greatly by gender and race, with elderly women having a higher poverty rate (16 percent) than men (9 percent). The poverty rate is higher for blacks (25 percent) and Hispanics (24 percent) than for whites (9 percent) (U.S. Bureau of the Census, 1996a).

Even though the elderly have experienced increased incomes in the past two decades, some elderly have not fared well. For example, in 1990, 12 percent of the elderly received major welfare assistance in an average month, compared with 8 percent of the population aged 18 to 64 (U.S. Bureau of the Census, 1996c). In Chapter 5, we examine the expenditures of elderly households across income levels, giving particular emphasis to poor elderly households.

Sources of Income

The composition of income of elderly households has changed dramatically, as highlighted in Table 2.3. The elderly rely much less on earnings, which are now only 18 percent of income versus 29 percent in 1967. Reliance on Social Security has increased from 34 percent to 42 percent. Social Security provided at least half of total income for 63 percent of beneficiaries in 1992. Also, it supplied nearly all income (90 percent or more) for 26 percent of the beneficiaries and was the only source of income for 14 percent of the beneficiaries (U.S. Bureau of the Census, 1996c). Although the increase in Social Security payments has been beneficial to current retirees, the rise in dependence on Social Security has some ominous implications when the baby boomers begin to retire in 2011. In a recent survey, only one-fourth of the adult population believed that when they retire, they will receive the level of benefits currently being received.[5] However, it is questionable whether these concerns will motivate persons approaching retirement to prepare contingency plans or to increase savings to compensate for smaller Social Security benefits.

Pension income, as a percent of total income, increased four percentage points over the 1967 to 1994 period, while asset income's share increased 3 percentage points (to 18 percent in 1994). Asset income is a much more volatile source of income due to fluctuations in the real estate and stock markets. Thus comparisons of asset income in any two years must be made with caution. In the 1980s, asset income was 26 to 28 percent of total income, but in 1994 assets only provided 18 percent of total income. Much of this decline in asset income in 1994 was due to a poor year for stock returns (the S&P 500 increased only 1.3 percent). Nonetheless, asset income is likely to continue to grow in importance. As revealed in Table 2.4, the elderly increased their real net assets dramatically (22 percent for the 65 to 74 age group), while the overall population experienced a 7.5 percent decline.[6] Given the importance of assets in providing long-term security, we include financial assets as an explanatory variable in our expenditure regression models in the following chapters.

Table 2.4
Assets and Liabilities by Age

Age	Means in 1993-94				Real Percent Change:1984-85 to 1993-94			
	Financial Assets	Real Estate	Total Liabilities	Net Assets	Financial Assets	Real Estate	Total Liabilities	Net Assets
All U.S.	$23,597	$68,824	$27,791	$64,630	16.9	-1.7	37.1	-7.5
55-64	39,523	105,380	25,330	119,573	5.5	6.4	77.2	-2.1
65-74	52,167	89,231	8,880	132,518	50.6	12.1	51.6	22.3
75 +	50,328	76,990	2,790	124,528	-17.3	18.1	62.5	0.2

Source: U.S. Dept. of Labor, Bureau of Labor Statistics, 1995, *Consumer expenditure survey: Quarterly data from the Interview Survey*, second quarter 1995, Report 907.

Retirement Savings

Even though the elderly have increased their net assets, Americans of all ages, including the elderly, are not saving enough for their retirement expectations. A recent survey[7] revealed that the average worker expects to receive a retirement income of $26,256 per year. Workers who are 60 years old and plan to retire at age 65 will need $353,254 in total savings, including Social Security, to fund this income. If the 60-year-old worker has $140,000 already saved, the worker needs to put away an additional $2,325 per *month* to retire at 65 on a $26,256 yearly income. But the survey found that the average worker at age 45 to 64 is saving only $2,529 per *year*.[8]

Retirement patterns and savings differ among occupations and industries. Operatives and laborers are more likely to leave the labor force at age 55 than are professionals, possibly due to the self-employed person's desire to accumulate savings to finance retirement (Hayward and Grady, 1990). Only 37 percent of workers in personal services industries and 34 percent in agriculture, forestry, and fisheries industries were covered by pension plans in 1991 (U.S. Bureau of the Census, 1996c). As a consequence, farm laborers are more likely to reenter the workforce after their first "retirement" than are workers in industries covered by pension plans. Although women have historically had relatively low pension incomes, they are more likely in the future to have pensions in their own names, which may reduce their desire or need to work after retirement. One indication of the improved prospects for pensions for women is the increase in the median years of employee tenure with current employer. Tenure for women age 45 to 54 years increased from 6 years in 1983 to 7 years in 1996. In contrast, during this same time period, median years of employee tenure with current employer for men age 45 to 54 years decreased from 13 years to 10 years (U.S. Department of Labor, 1997).

An increasing proportion of early pensioners have reentered the workforce since the 1970s. Half of men aged 55 to 61 and one-fourth of men aged 62 to 64 who were receiving pensions were still working (Herz, 1995). Improved health, increased life expectancies, loss of health insurance, and erosion of annuities due to inflation are contributing factors in the return of the "retiree" (Herz, 1995).

EXPENDITURES

Planning for retirement is an essential step for long-term financial stability. One component of this planning is recognition that expenses differ between elderly and nonelderly households. The U.S. Bureau of Labor Statistics 1995 Consumer Expenditure Survey reveals these differences (see Table 2.5). The most notable difference occurs in the area of health care expenses, but many other differences are significant as well. Elderly persons (over 65) spend roughly 12 percent on health care compared to only 5 percent for the overall population. Elderly persons also spend more on cash gifts and contributions, 5 percent versus 3 percent for the overall population. However, the elderly spend less on transportation (15 percent versus 19 percent), less on personal insurance and pensions (3.6 percent versus 9 percent), and less on apparel and services (3.9 percent versus 5.3 percent). While these figures provide a snapshot of the current situation of the expenditure shares of elderly households, they do not capture the dynamic changes over time or the differences across the heterogeneous population of the elderly. For this reason, Chapters 3 and 4 examine these temporal changes and variations in detail. We analyze changes in expenditures of the retired that occurred from the early 1970s to the mid-1980s, as well as differences in expenditures of the retired and nonretired. We also examine the major changes in expenditures that occur as persons enter retirement.

HEALTH ISSUES

Health is a major concern for every age group, but it is particularly important for the elderly. The demand for various health care services changes with age, and health care expenses generally increase with age. While health care expenses are examined in each of the next three chap-

Table 2.5
1995 Average Annual Expenditures and Shares by Age

	All Consumer Units		65 and over	
	Expenditure	Share	Expenditure	Share
Consumer unit characteristics				
Income before taxes	$36,918		$22,148	
Average number of persons	2.5		1.7	
Age of reference person	48		74.4	
Number of vehicles	1.9		1.4	
Total Expenditures	$32,264		$22,249	
Food	4,505	14.0	3,338	15.0
Alcoholic beverages	277		171	
Housing	10,458	32.4	7,585	34.1
Shelter	5,928	18.4	3,666	16.5
Owned dwellings	3,749	11.6	2,398	10.8
Rented dwellings	1,788	5.5	933	4.2
Other dwellings	391	1.2	335	1.5
Utilities, fuels, & public services	2,191	6.8	1,981	8.9
House furnishing & operations	2,340	7.3	1,939	8.7
Apparel and services	1,704	5.3	875	3.9
Transportation	6,014	18.6	3,374	15.2
Health care	1,732	5.4	2,648	11.9
Entertainment	1,612	5.0	926	4.2
Cash gifts and contributions	925	2.9	1,099	4.9
Personal insurance and pensions	2,964	9.2	799	3.6
Other expenses	2,073	6.4	1,434	6.4

Note: Other expenses include personal care products and services, reading, education, tobacco, and miscellaneous.

Source: U.S. Dept. of Labor, Bureau of Labor Statistics, 1996, *Consumer expenditure survey, 1995*, Table 3.

ters, Chapter 6 is specifically devoted to out-of-pocket health care expenditures. This section will briefly discuss the major health issues facing the elderly, such as the leading causes of mortality, health insurance and health care costs, and the need for personal assistance.

Mortality

In 1991 heart disease was still the leading cause of death among the elderly (597,000 deaths), while cancer (355,000 deaths) was second, and stroke (125,000 deaths) was third. Pneumonia, influenza, and chronic obstructive pulmonary diseases are also important causes of death. Further, as an elderly person ages, heart disease is much more likely to cause death. In 1991 heart disease was the cause of death in 44 percent of persons age 85 and older. Although heart disease is the primary cause of death in the elderly, significant reductions in the death rate have occurred since 1960, while death rates due to cancer have increased (National Center for Health Statistics, 1993).

Smoking has been associated with all three major causes of death (heart disease, malignant neoplasm, and cerebrovascular disease). Therefore, the purchase of smoking products is an important consumer and policy issue. Elderly men are more likely to smoke than women, and elderly black men have the highest percentage of smokers. However, in the past three decades smoking rates have fallen for men but have increased for women. In 1992, 15 percent of white males and 28 percent of black males smoked in comparison to 13 percent of white females and 11 percent of black females (National Center for Health Statistics, 1994). Because smoking is an important health issue, variations in tobacco expenditures across household types and time are examined in Chapters 3 and 4 in our expenditure regression models.

Alcohol consumption also has important health impacts. The lower mortality risk of light to moderate drinkers causes the alcohol-mortality curve to be J-shaped; mortality is lower for moderate drinkers compared to non-drinkers, but mortality increases significantly for heavy drinkers. Among current drinkers, elderly men are nearly twice as likely (14 percent) to be heavy drinkers (14 or more drinks per week) as elderly women (6 percent) (National Center for Health Statistics, 1994). Alcohol consumption generally declines with age. Variations in alcohol expenditures across household type and time are examined in our econometric models in Chapters 3 and 4. In particular, the effects of race, age, gender and income on alcohol consumption are estimated.

Until recently, suicide among the elderly was not a health issue that received intensive inquiry. But more recently researchers have investigated some of the perplexing issues such as why elderly white males have the highest suicide rates among the elderly. In fact, elderly white males are the only race/ethnic/gender group in the entire population more likely to commit suicide than to die in a motor vehicle accident (National Center for

Health Statistics, 1993). Because widowerhood and unemployment seem to statistically contribute to this higher suicide rate (McCall and Land, 1994), researchers have argued that elderly men need to rely more on relationships and less on work as coping strategies. Elderly women apparently have better coping strategies (Canetto, 1992).

Health Insurance and Health Care Costs

Health insurance coverage is a major concern for every person, particularly for the elderly. Currently, almost all of the elderly are covered. A longitudinal 32-month study starting in 1990 revealed that 99.4 percent of the elderly had continuous coverage through either private health insurance, Medicare, Medicaid, or military health care. Medicare was a much more important sole source of insurance for blacks (37 percent) and Hispanics (30 percent) than whites (13 percent) (Bennefield, 1994). Expenditures on health care insurance are examined in detail in Chapter 6, so here we only highlight some of the major issues.

An increasing proportion of public health care spending has flowed to the elderly. Policymakers are concerned about this trend, particularly with the first of the baby boomers reaching retirement age in 2011. In 1987, 58 percent of public health care dollars were spent on the elderly, compared to 51 percent in 1977. During this time frame, per capita public expenditures on personal health care for the elderly increased 49 percent (in constant 1987 dollars). Further, personal health care expenditures (in 1987) were strongly related to age, ranging from $3,700 for persons 65 to 69 years old to roughly $9,200 for persons 85 years and older (U.S. Bureau of the Census, 1996c).

Concerns are mounting about the solvency of Medicare, as the elderly move into the oldest old category (U.S. Council of Economic Advisors, 1997). Public funds paid for approximately two-thirds of the bill for the elderly (National Center for Health Statistics, 1994, table 145). In 1991, annual Medicare payments per person ranged from $2,700 for persons age 65 to 69 to $4,900 for persons 85 years and older. Similar concerns about Medicaid are mounting because the elderly represented only 12 percent of Medicaid recipients in 1992 but received nearly one-third of the Medicaid budget (National Center for Health Statistics, 1994, tables 148, 150).

The Need for Personal Assistance

The increased life expectancy and need for personal assistance require that families make numerous adjustments. Many persons in their fifties and sixties are likely to have surviving parents, aunts, and uncles, many of whom will live long enough to encounter multiple, chronic illnesses. One measure of this situation is the "parent-support" ratio—the number of persons 85 years and older per 100 persons age 50 to 64 years.[9] In 1950, when the parent-support ratio was 3, few persons had to worry about supporting older relatives. By 1993 the ratio had more than tripled to 10. It is expected that the parent-support ratio will rise to 29 by 2050, a tenfold increase over the course of a century (U.S. Bureau of the Census, 1996c).

When an elderly person shares a home with someone other than the spouse, it is usually with an adult daughter. Consequently, numerous women are not working outside the home during their parent-care years (U.S. Bureau of the Census, 1996c). This may explain in part the plateau in labor force participation rates of women in the 1990s.

The need for personal assistance with everyday activities (e.g., bathing, moving around the house, and preparing meals) increases with age. Only 9 percent of those age 65–69 need help, but fully half of those 85 and over need help. The proportion of elderly persons with two or more common chronic conditions (referred to as comorbidity) was higher for women than for men. Among persons age 80 years and older, 70 percent of women versus 53 percent of men had two or more chronic conditions (U.S. Bureau of the Census, 1996c).

Although the need for personal assistance is an extremely important issue, most Americans are not well informed about the risks and choices in long-term care. In a national survey conducted by John Hancock Mutual Life Insurance Company and the National Council on the Aging, American adults were asked 10 questions concerning the likelihood of needing long-term care and its cost. The average score was only 3 out of 10 correct.[10]

SUMMARY

Clearly the elderly are not a homogenous group. Their preferences and expenditures for various goods and services differ with respect to age, gender, race, income, and educational groups. These expenditure differences are important for decision making for both businesses and government policymakers. Further, the elderly population has undergone many transitions and continues to do so. Elderly persons are retiring earlier, living longer, and living more active lives. All of these changes have important ramifications for consumer expenditures, particularly as the elderly population share grows to as much as 20 percent by the middle of the next century. In the following chapters, we examine the differences in expenditures for various goods and services purchased by the elderly. Our expenditure models explicitly recognize the heterogeneity of this rapidly growing segment of the population by including explanatory variables that capture the unique differences in elderly household demographics (such as age, marital status, gender, race, income, and wealth). Our models compare elderly households across time, elderly to nonelderly households, and retired to nonretired elderly households.

NOTES

1. Seventy-five million babies (so-called baby boomers) were born in the United States between 1946 and 1964.

2. Life expectancies (at age 65) for black males and females are approximately two years less than that of their white counterparts.

3. Japan has the highest life expectancies at birth and at age 65. Life expectancy in Japan at age 65 is 16.5 for males and 20.6 for females.

4. In some of our models we include age as a continuous variable, and in other models we use age group as a dummy variable to measure the impact of age on expenditures.

5. The survey, titled "Empire State Survey on the Generations," was conducted in 1996 on 1,200 Americans (Associated Press, Dec. 9, 1996).

6. The U.S. Bureau of Labor Statistics CE Interview Survey data set does not contain information on the value of pensions nor the value of non-real-estate property. The calculation of pension values would be relatively straightforward for defined contribution plans, but the value of defined benefit plans depends on complicated present value formulas that may be too difficult for individuals to solve. Without this information the estimates of net assets cannot be completely assessed.

7. The survey, titled "Workplace Pulse," interviewed 1,000 full-time workers ("Survey," 1996).

8. John Penko, vice president for Colonial Life and Accident Insurance Company, notes, "That's a huge gap between what people expect and what they will likely receive" (Associated Press, Dec. 3, 1996).

9. This ratio is a crude measure, because persons in the age group in the numerator are not necessarily in the same families as those in the denominator.

10. For example, 86 percent of respondents underestimated the percentage of people who get long-term care in their homes, which is 80 percent; more than 60 percent did not know that two out of five people receiving long-term care are under the age of 65; nearly half of all respondents (48 percent) did not know that people have to spend all or almost all of their assets to get Medicaid benefits; 80 percent underestimated the average cost of a home visit by a visiting nurse, which is $100 per visit; and more than half (65 percent) reported that they had done little or nothing in the way of planning for their own long-term care needs (Texas Institute for Research & Education on Aging, 1997).

Chapter 3

Change in Expenditure Patterns

Retirees have become a major consumer group with considerable disposable income to satisfy their unique needs and wants. Businesses increasingly recognize the potential impact of this growing group of consumers.
In the U.S. free market economy, the major realization of desires and demands is through actual purchases and changes in expenditure patterns
over time.

Economic and social structures have changed significantly in the past
two decades, particularly for the elderly, who are living longer, more active
lives. Consequently, the expectations of society and older Americans have
changed. As age of retirement has declined and life span has lengthened,
retirees are encountering both the advantages and disadvantages associated
with an extended retirement period. They have more years to enjoy a new
lifestyle, but they also are concerned with issues such as financing a longer
period of retirement and possibly declining health.

This chapter presents a detailed comparative analysis of retired households to determine changes in their expenditure patterns and economic status from the early 1970s to the mid-1980s. This was a period of substantial
growth both of the elderly population and of the general economy, but with
relatively high inflation rates. We analyze major expenditures, income, savings, and taxes to examine relative changes in the decision making and the

economic status of older Americans during this period. Several expenditure areas—health care, leisure activities, necessities, and philanthropy—are of special importance in examining changes in retiree lifestyles. Tobit regressions are used to determine the effects of age, family type, education, race, income, and wealth on the expenditures of retirees.

DEMOGRAPHIC, ECONOMIC, AND POLICY CHANGES

In this section we briefly overview several of the significant economic and policy changes that affected the elderly. The 1972 to 1987 period was a time of rising real income for the elderly and a period during which numerous policies were implemented or changed. Double income tax deductions for personal exemptions were available in 1972, but not in 1987. Further, marginal tax rates declined during this period. More elderly persons were eligible for welfare in 1972 because Supplemental Security Income (SSI) did not exist. The Social Security Administration introduced automatic cost-of-living adjustments in 1972, but since 1984, higher-income Social Security beneficiaries have paid income tax on up to 50 percent of their benefits (Schulz, 1992). The Employee Retirement Income Security Act of 1974 (ERISA) assured earlier vesting and made private pensions more secure. Charitable giving was negatively impacted during this period by the implementation of the 1981 Economic Recovery Tax Act and the Tax Reform Act of 1986 (Clotfelter, 1985, 1989; Hopkins, 1982).

Retiree preferences were also affected by two important demographic shifts: longer life expectancies and lower male labor force participation rates. From 1970 to 1986, life expectancy of those reaching age 65 increased 13 percent (from 13 to 14.7 years) for males and 11 percent (from 16.8 to 18.6 years) for females. In addition, the male labor force participation rate declined from 83 to 67 percent for ages 55 to 64, and it fell from 27 to 16 percent for those age 65 and older (U.S. Bureau of the Census, 1989).

Health care inflation rates posed serious problems, as Medicare beneficiaries encountered substantial increases in their co-payments and deductibles. The increase in life expectancy and declining average age of entry into retirement increased the length of active retired life and affected spending on travel, leisure activities, and food away from home. The level of educational attainment of retirees increased as well. Further, businesses began to target the substantial discretionary spending of the retired (Lazer and Shaw, 1987; Longino, 1988; Moon, 1991). All of these policy and demographic changes influenced retiree consumption and lifestyles.

As discussed in Chapter 1, the two dominant theories of consumer behavior—the Life Cycle Hypothesis (Ando and Modigliani, 1963) and the

Permanent Income Hypothesis (Friedman, 1957)—suggest that consumers strive to smooth their spending over time by saving during their peak earning years and dissaving during retirement. However, Deaton (1992) suggested that a precautionary motive based on uncertainty regarding life span, health care costs, and poverty might make elderly persons cautious about reducing their assets. We address these issues in the study presented in the following sections, which was published in the *Journal of Gerontology*.[1]

EMPIRICAL ANALYSIS—DATA AND METHODOLOGY

Data

The data for this chapter are drawn from the U.S. Bureau of Labor Statistics Consumer Expenditure Survey, described in Chapter 1. The CE Survey categories comprise approximately 95 percent of total household spending (Gieseman, 1987), and include pension and social security contributions. We report pension and social security contributions but do not include them in total average expenditures nor in the calculation of expenditure shares. We excluded them in order to analyze discretionary spending decisions and to compare the propensities to consume for various categories of expenditures.

Cross-sectional data are from the CE interview surveys for 1972–1973 (referred to as 1972 in this chapter) and for 1986 and 1987 (and referred to as 1987 in this chapter), which are pooled to enhance sample size.[2] Files containing consumption expenditures, income sources, selected financial assets, taxes, and demographic data were developed for retired households over age 50 for the two time periods. We chose age 50 to include early retirees of the 1980s. The data are limited to complete income reporters who are either single-person or married-couple households, with no others present in either case. For 1987, data are limited to the fifth interview, which is the only one that contains complete household income and asset data. The data files exclude households with wage and salary or unemployment compensation income. Because the CE categories for race changed between the 1972 survey and the 1987 survey, the data were regrouped to develop comparable categories of black and non-black based on the 1972 designations. Using the Consumer Price Index (CPI), all 1972 dollars are inflated to 1987 price levels.[3]

The data measure expenditures, not consumption per se. Since no data adjustment is made for the contribution of durables to household consumption or the estimation of current-year depreciation, then it is appropriate to examine propensities to "spend" rather than propensities to "consume" (Fareed and Riggs, 1982; Danziger et al., 1982–83). The importance of this distinction is heightened because households, especially elderly households, may have inventories of goods that they can draw down and that affect current consumption but not expenditure. Thus the coefficient on income (in our expenditure models) measures the marginal propensity to spend (MPC),[4] not the marginal propensity to consume. Although all of the demographic variables are important explanatory variables, the MPC is particularly significant because it indicates the share of an additional dollar of income that would be allotted to each expenditure category.

Methodology

Descriptive statistics are used first to compare the values and budget shares of expenditures on 27 different BLS-defined categories of goods for various types of households. Then two-stage Tobit regressions are developed to examine the change in patterns of elderly household expenditures. There are two statistical reasons these methods are used. First, Tobit regressions are needed because the dependent variable is censored (i.e., expenditures for some households on some items can be zero), which would bias ordinary least squares estimators. Second, since permanent income is unobservable, we have an errors in variables problem. Since transitory factors have a relatively small impact on expenditures, permanent income is represented by total expenditures. Thus, a two-stage estimator must be used in conjunction with the Tobit model. The model and estimation method are presented in the appendix to this chapter.

This methodology is also applied in Chapter 4, with only minor variations. In general the explanatory variables are income, family status, race, educational attainment, age, and financial assets. Household type, race, education, and age are measured using dummy variables. Household type uses a base case of a single female and different dummy variables for single males and married couples. The race dummy variable uses a black person as the base case. For education, less than a high school education is the base case; three education dummy variables are created for persons with high school, college, and more than college educations. For the age variable, the base case is a person less than age 60, and the age dummy variables are age 60 to 64, age 65 to 74, and age 75 and over.

Although all of the explanatory variables are important, income is an especially significant variable. Thus for each of the expenditure categories, we calculate the marginal propensity to spend (MPC) as described above. The MPC is given by the value of the permanent income coefficient, which indicates the share of an additional dollar of income that would be allotted to that category. We also calculate the expenditure elasticities, indicating the percentage change in expenditure on an item in response to a 1 percent change in total expenditure, for each consumption item. (See the appendix to this chapter.) If the calculated elasticity for a specific item is greater than one, it is termed a luxury good, and its budget share will increase as income increases. If the elasticity is less than one, it indicates that the budget share for the item will decrease as income increases.

Summary Statistics

Considerable change occurred in education levels of the elderly between 1972 and 1987. The portion reporting at least a high school education increased from about one-third to almost half, and the share reporting a college education increased by 10 percent. All family types had increases in home ownership, with the largest increases for single males, followed by single females, as couples already had 80 percent ownership in 1972. The share of homeowners without a mortgage increased for single owners but decreased for couples. This may reflect the greater likelihood of married couples moving to a new or different residence and undertaking a new mortgage at or near retirement, whereas single retirees were more likely to remain at the same location.

Income and Assets

Income and assets of retired households in 1972 (in 1987 dollars) and in 1987 were analyzed by family type (see Table 3.1). Real after-tax income rose for married couples (7 percent) and for single males (12 percent), but single females experienced an 11 percent drop. Inflation averaged a high 6.7 percent annually (U.S. Bureau of the Census, 1989), which contributed to the stagnation of real income (U.S. Council of Economic Advisors, 1988; Levy, 1987).

All three household groups experienced substantial declines in their financial assets over the 15-year period. Assets of married couples and single females declined to about half the 1972 levels, and assets of single males declined to three-quarters of the 1972 level. Also reported assets declined for all age categories, except single males age 50 to 64. This is consistent with the general declines in savings rates (discussed later in this chapter) and real incomes of 1987 retirees in their preretirement years. The mean number of vehicles approximately doubled for each group, reinforcing the perception of their increased interest in leisure and travel and

Table 3.1
Income and Assets of Retired Households (Age 50+):
1972 and 1987 (1987 Dollars)

	Married		Single Male		Single Female	
	1972	1987	1972	1987	1972	1987
Income by source	(n=838)	(n=586)	(n=335)	(n=216)	(n=943)	(n=681)
Non-farm business	0.8	0.6	0.0	0.0	0.3	0.0
Social security/ RRR	49.0	48.4	52.3	46.8	43.4	57.7
SSI	0.0	0.5	0.0	1.9	0.0	1.4
Dividends, royalties	6.9	8.3	5.0	8.6	10.5	8.2
Interest	12.8	13.8	12.1	15.1	13.3	10.3
Pensions & annuities	17.7	25.7	12.1	23.4	12.1	16.8
Welfare	1.3	0.1	3.6	0.4	4.1	0.2
Workmen's comp.	4.8	1.2	7.1	2.3	4.6	1.3
Other	6.6	1.5	10.8	1.4	11.9	4.1
Income before tax	$17,250	$18,584	$9,808	$11,133	$9,990	$8,698
Income after tax	$16,493	$17,636	$9,632	$10,813	$9,430	$8,392
Avg. Propen. to Cons.	94.4%	97.6%	86.2%	104.5%	97.4%	112.9%
Value of selected assets						
Checking accounts	$2,499	$3,110	$1,159	$3,040	$1,378	$1,199
Savings accounts	$26,861	$16,221	$16,148	$10,551	$14,418	$6,303
Stocks and bonds	$22,573	$8,277	$5,858	$3,793	$7,637	$3,496
U.S. Govt. bonds	$2,569	$941	$915	$273	$903	$224
Total Selected Assets	$54,501	$28,549	$24,080	$17,657	$24,337	$11,222

Source: M. Nieswiadomy and R. M. Rubin, 1995, Changes in expenditure patterns of retirees: 1972–73 and 1986–87, *Journal of Gerontology: Social Sciences*, 50B(5):
S274–S290. Reprinted by permission of The Gerontological Society of America.

greater mobility. It appears that 1987 retirees preferred to hold more cars
and less financial assets than those of 15 years earlier.

Expenditures

Major expenditure categories and shares were compared for the three
household types, the total sample, and over time, as shown in Table 3.2. All
groups revealed a lower propensity to save, with a dramatic increase in the
overall average propensity to consume (APC) from 90 percent in 1972 to
103 percent in 1987. The jump for single females was even greater—from
92 percent to 113 percent. The increase in APC occurred for all age groups.

Several economic factors that changed substantially over the period may
have affected budget shares. For example, the relative prices of goods

Table 3.2
Average Annual Expenditure Shares of Retired Households:
1972 and 1987

	Married Couple		Single Male		Single Female	
	1972	1987	1972	1987	1972	1987
Food	22.9	18.6	25.5	17.6	20.8	16.6
Food at home	20.0	12.3	19.0	10.7	18.3	11.8
Food away from home	2.9	5.8	6.5	6.3	2.5	3.9
Alcoholic beverage	0.6	1.1	1.7	1.9	0.3	0.5
Housing	29.1	29.7	33.7	29.5	40.2	42.9
Shelter	14.8	14.9	20.8	16.4	23.2	22.7
Owned dwelling	9.2	9.4	6.0	6.1	8.8	10.2
Rented dwelling	4.0	3.3	13.7	9.2	13.1	11.2
Other dwelling	1.6	2.2	1.0	1.1	1.4	1.3
Utilities, fuels & pub. serv.	8.9	9.4	8.7	8.7	10.5	12.3
Household operations	1.9	1.6	2.2	1.5	3.5	3.8
House furnishing & equip.	3.6	3.8	2.0	2.9	3.0	4.0
Apparel and services	5.1	3.7	5.1	2.6	6.0	3.9
Transportation	15.7	17.5	11.4	22.2	9.3	9.8
Vehicles	4.7	6.0	2.3	11.3	2.3	1.8
Gasoline & motor oil	4.2	4.0	3.3	4.4	2.1	2.3
Other vehicle	5.5	5.7	3.9	5.3	3.2	4.0
Public transportation	1.2	1.9	1.9	1.2	1.8	1.8
Health care	9.7	12.1	7.5	9.5	9.0	11.3
Entertainment	2.7	4.2	4.5	2.9	1.8	2.7
Personal care	1.6	1.3	1.0	0.6	1.8	1.6
Reading	0.6	0.8	0.6	0.8	0.7	0.9
Education	0.2	0.1	0.1	0.0	0.2	0.0
Tobacco	1.2	1.0	1.7	1.4	0.6	0.7
Miscellaneous	0.3	2.3	0.3	5.7	0.5	3.1
Cash gifts and contributions	8.4	6.0	6.0	4.5	7.8	5.3
Life & personal insurance	1.9	1.6	1.0	1.0	1.1	0.8
Total avg. expend. (1987$)	$15,575	$17,216	$8,298	$11,297	$9,181	$9,477

Source: M. Nieswiadomy and R. M. Rubin, 1995, Changes in expenditure patterns of retirees: 1972–1973 and 1986–1987, *Journal of Gerontology: Social Sciences*,
50B(5): S274–290. Reprinted by permission of the Gerontological Society of
America.

changed during the period. While overall prices, as measured by the CPI,
increased 171 percent from 1972 to 1987, six items had much lower rates
of price increase: alcohol (119 percent), apparel (77 percent), vehicles (109
percent), entertainment (123 percent), household operations (115 percent),
and house furnishings (115 percent). Three categories had substantially

more rapid inflation: health care (248 percent), education (290 percent), and new houses (233 percent). Utilities (216 percent) and public transportation (208 percent) also had fairly rapid price increases.

Food expenditure shares fell for all three groups, decreasing most for males. The share (and real dollar amounts) spent on alcohol increased for all groups, but it remained less than .5 percent for single women and rose to 2 percent for single men. Since the relative price of alcohol was lower, this indicates that the quantity of alcohol purchased increased. Whether this increase was due to lower prices or preference changes (or both) we cannot say. Interestingly, even as expenditure on alcohol was increasing, the desire of older retirees to purchase alcohol, relative to their younger cohorts, went down by $283 annually, as discussed in the Tobit regression results section.

The share of total expenditure allocated to housing remained the same for married couples, declined for single men, and rose for single women. The very large share of spending (43 percent by 1987) allocated to housing by retired females is notable, particularly when compared to the 30 percent housing expenditure share for couples and single males. The budget shares and expenditures for apparel declined for all three retired groups.[5] The transportation share increased only slightly for married couples and single females, but it doubled for single males, who appear to have increased their mobility much more than other retirees. Since single males greatly increased their budget share for vehicle purchases, it is somewhat surprising that their expenditure share on entertainment declined. This was not the case for married couples or single females, who allocated more to entertainment in 1987.

We also analyzed the change in expenditure shares, stratified by age, as shown in Table 3.3. Changes in budget shares varied greatly across the age groups, particularly for health care, cash gifts, and transportation. Health care expenditures, including insurance premiums, increased by about two percentage points and in 1987 ranged from 10 percent for single males to 12 percent for married couples. This may have been caused by the increase in health care costs. However, the increases in budget shares were much larger for the older age group, and the range in health care budget shares for the various age groups is much larger in 1987. This may be due to younger retirees being more likely to receive employer-provided retirement health benefits, which have dramatically increased, or to increased desire of the oldest old to purchase health care (Schulz, 1992). The share for gifts and contributions declined for all groups, possibly due to lower marginal tax rates, as discussed next. In general, the younger old (under age 85) allocated greater budget shares to transportation in 1987 than in 1972.

Table 3.3
Average Annual Expenditure Shares of Retired Households by Age:
1972 and 1987

	1972					1987				
Age:	50-59	60-64	65-74	75-84	85+	50-59	60-64	65-74	75-84	85+
Sample size:	(85)	(164)	(956)	(781)	(130)	(71)	(164)	(608)	(533)	(107)
Food	20.2	21.9	21.9	23.4	22.0	19.0	18.3	17.8	16.5	19.8
Food at home	17.4	18.6	18.3	20.9	17.3	11.3	11.9	12.0	11.4	15.2
Food away from home	2.8	3.2	3.6	2.6	4.7	5.7	5.1	5.7	4.1	4.1
Alcoholic beverage	1.1	0.9	0.7	0.4	0.3	1.8	1.2	1.1	0.6	0.5
Housing	36.6	31.6	33.3	36.5	41.3	35.1	37.5	33.1	36.7	46.0
Shelter	20.8	16.7	18.7	21.2	20.2	18.9	20.8	16.3	20.0	24.0
Owned dwelling	9.5	8.8	8.6	8.3	8.1	10.8	12.4	8.7	9.2	5.1
Rented dwelling	9.9	6.9	8.3	12.0	10.3	6.9	7.0	5.8	9.1	17.8
Other dwelling	1.5	1.0	1.8	0.9	1.8	1.3	1.4	1.8	1.7	1.1
Util, fuels & pub. serv	9.2	9.1	9.1	10.1	11.1	9.8	10.1	10.2	11.0	14.1
Household operations	2.2	1.9	2.2	2.7	7.8	1.2	1.5	2.5	2.9	5.1
House furn. & equip.	4.4	4.0	3.2	2.5	2.2	5.2	5.1	4.0	2.9	2.7
Apparel and services	7.3	6.2	5.9	4.7	4.5	3.2	4.3	4.1	3.1	2.0
Transportation	12.6	16.1	14.6	8.5	5.4	20.9	14.3	16.1	13.6	3.9
Vehicles	2.6	7.0	4.2	1.4	0.7	9.6	3.8	4.6	5.2	0.0
Gasoline & motor oil	3.6	3.5	3.8	2.2	1.1	4.3	3.9	3.8	2.5	1.6
Other vehicle	4.4	4.6	4.9	3.4	1.9	6.3	5.4	5.4	4.3	1.6
Public transportation	1.9	0.9	1.7	1.5	1.7	0.7	1.2	2.3	1.7	0.7
Health care	8.7	8.6	8.3	10.1	9.9	7.1	7.4	10.8	13.7	16.2
Entertainment	1.9	2.8	3.0	2.1	2.0	3.5	3.8	4.0	2.3	2.0
Personal care	1.5	1.3	1.6	1.5	1.6	0.8	1.2	1.3	1.4	1.6
Reading	0.6	0.6	0.6	0.7	0.9	0.8	0.8	0.9	0.8	0.8
Education	0.0	0.5	0.2	0.1	0.4	0.3	0.0	0.1	0.0	0.0
Tobacco	2.4	1.6	1.2	0.5	0.4	1.9	1.3	1.0	0.6	0.9
Miscellaneous	0.7	1.0	0.3	0.3	0.4	2.0	2.9	4.0	2.5	1.9
Cash gifts and contrib.	4.6	5.2	6.7	10.1	10.0	1.9	5.0	4.8	7.3	3.7
Life/personal insur.	1.9	1.8	1.7	1.0	0.9	1.7	1.9	1.1	1.0	0.5
Avg. prop. to cons. (%)	100.3	91.3	92.4	90.7	73.6	124.8	119.0	107.9	102.2	91.2
Total expend. (1987$)	12,008	12,817	12,749	10,287	8,803	13,384	15,478	13,873	11,695	7,713

Source: M. Nieswiadomy and R. M. Rubin, 1995, Changes in expenditure patterns of retirees 1972–1973 and 1986–1987, *Journal of Gerontology: Social Sciences*,
50B(5): S274–S290. Reprinted by permission of The Gerontological Society of
America.

Spending patterns of the 85+ group differ from those of the younger age
groups, consistent with Moehrle's (1990) findings. The expenditure shares
on housing are greatest for the oldest age group (85+) in both periods for
whom transportation and entertainment expenditure shares are notably
smaller.

Table 3.4 presents expenditure shares by income groups, using four income categories based on the federal poverty level and three higher-income groups delineated by Moehrle (1990). The intertemporal expenditure share changes were quite similar for most of the income groups for all three household types, but there were some differences. Shares for food, apparel, and cash gifts generally decreased over time. Health care shares generally increased for all three family types at all income levels except for the highest income group. Entertainment shares generally increased for all three family types at all income levels.

Saving and Dissaving

We find a dramatic shift in the savings out of current income when we compare mean after-tax income with total average expenditures. This holds for all three household types and over time. In 1972, positive saving from income was 10 percent for married couples, 16 percent for single males, 8 percent for single females, and 10 percent for all retired households. In contrast, by 1987, only married couples had positive savings, which had fallen to only 2 percent of after-tax income, or one-fourth the earlier level. Both single-male and single-female households were dissaving; and single females spent 13 percent more than their income. This finding highlights an important shift in retiree consumption behavior over time. Dissaving, which was not characteristic of retiree consumption patterns in 1972, was the predominant effect for single retirees 15 years later.

We find interesting implications for testing the Permanent Income Hypothesis in our APC results across the age groups, as the APC is smaller for older age groups (during 1972 and 1987) for married couples and single females (see Table 3.3). This finding is not consistent with the Permanent Income Hypothesis, but other researchers have also found that elderly household behavior does not conform closely to the Permanent Income Hypothesis (Danziger et al., 1982–83; Davies, 1981; Hogarth, 1989; Hurd, 1987; Mirer, 1979, 1980; Schwenk, 1990a; Stoller and Stoller, 1987; Torrey and Taeuber, 1986; Walker and Schwenk, 1991; Wilcox, 1991). This finding may lend credence to Deaton's (1992) precautionary theory of savings of the elderly. We turn next to our Tobit regression results to analyze consumption patterns for retirees.

Tobit Expenditure Regression Results

Table 3.5 presents the MPCs for 24 of the major expenditure categories.[6] Table 3.6 presents the Tobit regression coefficients and summary statistics

Table 3.4
Average Annual Expenditure Shares of Retired Households by After-Tax Income (1987 Dollars): 1972 and 1987

	1972				1987			
	Less than $7,372 (n=547)	$7,373 to $14,999 (n=1036)	$15,000 to $29,999 (n=413)	$30,000 or more (n=120)	Less than $7,372 (n=410)	$7,373 to $14,999 (n=717)	$15,000 to $29,999 (n=269)	$30,000 or more (n=87)
Food	28.0	23.6	20.7	16.0	19.7	18.3	17.3	13.9
Alcoholic beverage	0.3	0.6	0.7	0.7	0.7	0.8	1.1	1.6
Housing	39.1	35.4	31.3	29.9	39.4	36.5	32.5	28.1
Apparel and services	5.0	5.4	5.6	6.1	3.1	3.4	4.4	3.8
Transportation	8.4	11.6	15.6	14.3	10.5	14.8	15.6	21.4
Health care	8.8	9.8	9.1	7.3	12.7	11.8	12.0	7.2
Entertainment	1.7	2.6	3.1	2.6	2.9	2.6	3.6	6.4
Personal care	1.3	1.6	1.7	1.6	1.2	1.3	1.4	1.2
Reading & Education	0.6	0.8	0.9	1.1	0.8	0.9	1.0	0.8
Tobacco	1.3	1.1	1.0	0.6	1.3	1.1	0.7	0.5
Miscellaneous	0.3	0.4	0.6	0.2	3.2	3.6	1.7	3.2
Cash gifts & contributions	3.9	5.9	7.9	17.7	3.3	3.7	7.6	10.9
Life & personal insurance	1.3	1.3	1.7	1.9	1.3	1.2	1.1	1.2
Total average expenditure	$6,500	$10,268	$16,420	$29,293	$8,511	$11,127	$18,250	$29,956

Source: R. M. Rubin and M. Nieswiadomy, 1992, Changes in expenditure patterns of the retired: 1972–73 and 1986–87, Paper presented at 67th Annual Conference of the Western Economic Association International, San Francisco, July 10, 1992.

Table 3.5
Tobit Regression Estimates of the Marginal Propensity to Consume (MPC) of Retired Households (Age 50+): 1972 and 1987

Category	1972	1987	Category	1972	1987
Food	0.098 *	0.100 *	Health care	0.072 *	0.050 *
Food at home	0.045 *	0.045 *			
Food away	0.034 *	0.051 *	Entertainment	0.007	0.028 *
Alcoholic beverage	0.004 *	0.011 *	Personal care	0.010 *	0.009 *
Housing	0.352 *	0.191 *	Tobacco	0.001 *	0.001
Shelter	0.179 *	0.104 *			
Owned dwelling	0.109 *	0.059 *	Miscellaneous	0.003 *	0.051 *
Rented dwelling	-0.011	-0.002			
Other dwelling	0.019 *	0.008 *	Gifts/contribut.	0.189 *	0.103 *
Utilities/services	0.061 *	0.016 *			
House operations	0.032 *	0.021 *	Life insurance	0.007 *	0.003 *
House furnishing	0.029 *	0.050 *			
Apparel & services	0.032 *	0.053 *			
Transportation	0.048 *	0.174 *			
Gasoline & oil	0.013 *	0.013 *			
Other vehicle	0.031 *	0.050 *			
Public transport.	0.006 *	0.012 *			

*Statistically significant at $p < 0.10$.

Source: M. Nieswiadomy and R. M. Rubin, 1995, Changes in expenditure patterns of retirees: 1972–1973 and 1986–1987, *Journal of Gerontology: Social Sciences*, 50B(5): S274–S290. Reprinted by permission of The Gerontological Society of America.

for the four largest BLS-defined expenditure categories for 1972 and 1987. Expenditures on the major categories of food, housing, transportation, and health care comprise over three-quarters of retiree household spending. In addition, Table 3.7 presents the results for the leisure categories of food away from home, other vehicle expenses, public transportation, and entertainment.[7] The regressions utilize two continuous independent variables (permanent income and financial assets) and dummy variables for the sociodemographic variables of household type, race, education level, and age group. The base case is a single black female, in age group 50–59, with eight years or less of education. The appendix to Chapter 3 gives the details of the econometric methodology.

Although only eight detailed models are presented in Tables 3.6 and 3.7, the Chow tests, comparing the regressions for 1972 and 1987, indicate a significant difference, at the .01 level, for all 24 expenditure categories. Retirees in 1987 had very different expenditure functions than their 1972 counterparts, which is confirmed by the Chow tests. In this section we examine some of the differences in the expenditure functions over time, by comparing the coefficients of the sociodemographic variables.

Major Expenditure Categories. The coefficients in the expenditure function for total food revealed minimal change over the study period. As retirees shifted their spending preferences toward more leisure activities, the MPCs and income elasticities fell over this time period for housing and the subcategories of shelter, owned dwelling, and other dwelling. Housing expenditures may be less important for those who travel more often. The slightly higher percentage of homes owned without a mortgage may also play some role in the decline in the housing MPC. The effect of housing prices is difficult to ascertain because long-term mortgage payments depend on both the price and interest rate at the time of purchase. Nonetheless, a new home became 23 percent more expensive by 1987 (in 1987 dollars). Housing is a particularly important commodity for single females, consistent with the budget shares depicted in Table 3.2. Single females spent larger amounts on housing and all subcategories of housing than single males or married couples, ceteris paribus, and the difference widened over time. (The male dummy coefficient changed from –$600 to –$1,106, as shown in Table 3.6.) The level of education did not significantly affect overall housing expenditures in 1972, but higher education did positively impact spending on housing and other dwellings in 1987, and negatively impacted owned dwelling spending in 1972. Also, there is very little impact of race on housing at the aggregate level, but non-blacks spend more on owned dwelling and household operations and less on rented dwellings in 1987 than blacks, ceteris paribus.

Retirees' desire for transportation increased substantially over time, as seen in Table 3.6. Transportation cost does not appear to be a major factor, because its relative cost did not change substantially (transportation costs fell only 3 percent in 1987 dollars). The MPC for transportation tripled and the expenditure elasticity more than doubled, indicating that the retired developed a much stronger preference for transportation and increased mobility. Both couples and single males spent more on transportation than single females in 1972, but by 1987, only single males did. Both groups also purchased more gas and oil and incurred other vehicle expenses, consistently showing that single females are less mobile.

The retiree MPC for health care declined slightly over time. In particular, the income elasticity declined to approximately one half its 1972 level,

Table 3.6
Tobit Expenditure Regressions for Major Expenditure Categories: 1972 and 1987

	Food		Housing		Transportation		Health Care	
	1972	1987	1972	1987	1972	1987	1972	1987
Constant	781.19 *	419.09	521.56 *	2249.30 *	-1233.30 *	-2860.50 *	-430.43	-1171.50 *
Permanent Income	0.103 *	0.11 *	0.37 *	0.21 *	0.07 *	0.29 *	0.09 *	0.07 *
Elasticity	0.46	0.59	1.03	0.55	0.35	0.84	0.73	0.36
Married Couple	1000.8 *	722.52 *	-1337.60 *	-619.40 *	1555.10 *	1007.10	172.67 *	544.74 *
Single Male	299.33 *	215.82	-600.37 *	-1106.00 *	592.11 *	1866.20 *	-174.96	-155.81
Race (non-black)	-30.35	40.61	-45.25	-162.93	701.40 *	886.99	337.73	521.12 *
Education (High School)	-28.8	-32.67	132.13	154.22	501.18 *	-225.92	-69.99	244.90
Education (College)	43.4	276.87	-220.08	912.01 *	584.33 *	-78.22	116.48	-145.36
Education (College+)	0.998	-460.94	-357.79	1169.50 *	989.68 *	-336.87	-337.17 *	-173.12
Age (60-64)	289.98	102.6	-529.88	327.91	523.74	-978.42	115.15	154.30
Age (65-74)	272.92	124.91	-205.78	-434.30	99.53	-623.85	79.39	848.02 *
Age (75+)	143.23	-214.93	129.78	-295.30	-1080.40 *	-1218.70	255.53 *	1174.90 *
Assets	0.0001	-0.0016	-0.0034 *	-0.0037	0.0031 *	-0.0036	-0.0016 *	0.0018
Likelihood Ratio Test	586.2 *	418.88 *	665.26 *	207.64 *	468.54 *	162.88 *	385.44 *	134.00 *
Log-Likelihood	-6538.65	-4852.41	-7298.69	-14107.16	-7153.41	-6143.80	-5933.77	-12918.74
Chow Test	182.5 *		362.76 *		888.84 *		928.62 *	
Φ	0.95	0.91	0.95	0.91	0.65	0.60	0.80	0.72
Limit Observations	0	0	0	2	474	248	102	87

*Statistically significant at p<0.10.

Source: M. Nieswiadomy and R. M. Rubin, 1995, Changes in expenditure patterns of retirees: 1972–1973 and 1986–1987, *Journal of Gerontology: Social Sciences*, 50B(5): S274–S290. Reprinted by permission of The Gerontological Society of America.

Table 3.7
Tobit Expenditure Regressions for Leisure Categories: 1972 and 1987

	Food away		Other Vehicle Exp.		Public Transportation		Entertainment	
	1972	1987	1972	1987	1972	1987	1972	1987
Constant	-2231.60 *	-1701.10 *	-1600.10 *	-1743.60 *	-504.12 *	-2759.80 *	-1297.90 *	-1602.10 *
Permanent Income	0.09 *	0.09 *	0.07 *	0.10 *	0.02 *	0.06 *	0.02	0.06 *
Elasticity	1.02	0.87	0.72	1.02	0.35	0.44	0.14	0.53
Married Couple	-152.35	69.60 *	873.71 *	429.35 *	-324.85 *	-798.45 *	324.88 *	201.11 *
Single Male	714.45 *	338.53 *	431.75 *	493.34 *	7.44 *	-356.59 *	339.29	-88.05
Race (non-black)	792.01 *	626.81 *	501.21 *	391.32 *	-179.00 *	-954.65 *	580.72 *	681.17 *
Education (High School)	201.85 *	170.79	214.13 *	147.66	159.02 *	403.60	299.56 *	99.03
Education (College)	133.40	372.03	328.01 *	156.00	165.11	1412.20 *	773.86 *	297.11 *
Education (College+)	-38.56	-132.44	13.37	-16.02	399.50 *	673.95	596.88 *	646.25
Age (60-64)	89.69	-27.21	22.99	99.48	-149.50	4.82	126.99	-30.12
Age (65-74)	98.84	101.95	-37.16	139.11	69.31	160.36	187.37	-28.16
Age (75+)	-189.74	-199.67	-501.05	-160.15	-22.48 *	20.31	-15.68	-421.96 *
Assets	0.0004	-0.0001	0.0002	-0.0021	0.0000 *	0.0047 *	0.0011 *	0.0047 *
Likelihood Ratio Test	354.90 *	251.52 *	539.80 *	320.16 *	133.14 *	98.32 *	162.46 *	216.30 *
Log-Likelihood	-5886.48	-4663.09	-5908.93	-4511.99	-1688.14	-4010.30	-12918.74	-8946.26
Chow Test	212.54 *		109.34 *		692.72 *		154.56 *	
Φ	0.39	0.55	0.47	0.53	0.30	0.20	0.48	0.47
Limit Observations	1099	497	949	586	1372	1102	556	512

*Statistically significant at p<0.10.

Source: M. Nieswiadomy and R. M. Rubin, 1995, Changes in expenditure patterns of retirees: 1972–1973 and 1986–1987, *Journal of Gerontology: Social Sciences*, 50B(5): S274–S290. Reprinted by permission of The Gerontological Society of America.

which reveals that health care became more of a necessity. Married couples and non-blacks have significantly higher health care expenditures than single women and blacks, in both time periods, ceteris paribus. Also, age became a more influential determinant of health care spending. Retirees age 65 to 74 spent more on health care in both periods (relative to age 50 to 59, the base case), but those age 75+ displayed different patterns in the two periods, with lower spending in 1972 and higher spending in 1987. This is revealed in the much larger coefficients on the dummy variables for ages 65–74 and 75+. In fact, the coefficient on the dummy variable for age 75+ increased from $256 (in 1972) to $1,175 (in 1987). Increased life expectancy and new medical technologies are likely contributing factors in the increased medical spending of the oldest old. Health care expenditure patterns are examined in greater detail in Chapter 6.

Leisure Activities. Retirees in the mid-1980s became more willing to spend additional income on recreational activities than 15 years earlier. This is substantiated when we sum the MPCs for several leisure-type categories, including food away from home, other vehicle expenses, public transportation, and entertainment, as shown in Table 3.7. In 1972 the sum of these MPCs was 0.07, indicating that a household would spend approximately seven cents of an additional dollar on leisure. By 1987 this sum of MPCs for leisure pursuits had doubled to 0.14.

Although the MPC on food at home did not change over this 15-year period, the MPC on food away from home increased. This indicates that retirees had a greater proclivity to spend on eating out in 1987. Since the relative price of food away from home did not change during this study period, this notable shift appears to be a preference change. Not surprisingly, single males consume more food away from home than single females in both time periods. However, we find that the difference narrowed, as males spent only $339 more in 1987 compared to $714 more in 1972, indicating that female preference for dining out increased. Non-blacks spend more on food away from home than blacks in both periods.

We include other vehicle expenses as a leisure category because these expenses reveal greater use of owned vehicles and include rental expenses.[8] The MPC for other vehicle expenses rose from 0.03 to 0.05, and the income elasticity increased from 0.72 to 1.02, indicating a shift toward a luxury good category.

Public transportation includes both intercity and intracity transit. For retirees who are not commuting to work, the use of intracity public transportation is expected to decline, so that much of their public transportation expenditure reflects leisure travel. The marginal propensity to spend on public transportation increased substantially over the time period. This finding that older Americans spend more on travel is clearly connected to the increased MPC on food away from home, discussed earlier.

The entertainment MPC increased from zero to .03, and the income elasticity increased from 0.17 to 0.53, revealing the greater activity of retirees. The lower relative price of entertainment may also have contributed to the increase in its income elasticity. Non-blacks had higher entertainment expenditures in both periods.

Alcohol and Tobacco. Expenditures on alcohol and tobacco have important health ramifications for older Americans. Retirees spent more on alcohol in 1987 than in the early 1970s, in terms of both dollar amount and expenditure share. Also, the MPC for alcohol more than tripled, which may be due to its real price decline of 20 percent or to preference changes. Couples and single males spent more on alcohol than single females in both time periods. The impact of age on alcohol purchases shifted; in 1972, the age 60–64 and 75 and over retirees consumed more alcohol than younger (50–59) retirees, ceteris paribus, but by 1987 age had a negative impact on alcohol consumption. This may indicate increased health awareness of older retirees over time.

While married couples and single males spent more on tobacco than single females, race is not a significant determinant of smoking. Older age groups spent significantly less on tobacco in both periods. The coefficients seem to be similar across time, but the intercept is lower, which may be another indicator of older retirees' increased health consciousness.

Gifts and Contributions. One notable finding is the tremendous decline over time in the MPC for cash gifts and contributions. This may have been caused by substantially lower tax rates or lower financial assets and savings in 1987. In both periods, single females gave more than either couples or single males. This may be related to the finding that couples were more likely to purchase life and personal insurance than single females. Blacks spent more on cash gifts and contributions and more on life and personal insurance than non-blacks in 1987. The regression coefficient for assets in 1987 was positive and significant. The oldest old (75+) continued to give substantially more over time than the younger old.

CONCLUSIONS

Our analysis of retiree expenditure share changes over time highlights major trends and lifestyle changes of retired Americans. Significant shifts in expenditure patterns developed over the 15-year period.

Health care expenditures increased in importance, as the retired are spending more out-of-pocket for health care. As we indicate in Chapter 6, this relates to greatly increased health insurance premiums. In addition, the findings show an increased desire for medical care because real expenditures on health care increased more than the real cost of health care. Health care costs increased 28 percent (in 1987 dollars), but couples spent 38 percent more, single males spent 72 percent more, and single females spent 30 percent more. The finding that health care spending was much more positively correlated with age in 1987 than in 1972 indicates increased use of health services and advanced medical technology in the latter stages of life. While real expenditures on health have increased, the income elasticity has decreased, indicating that it will be difficult to control health care costs as demand for health services becomes less income elastic.

As anticipated, retiree preferences for leisure activities increased substantially over time as their spending patterns shifted. Single males and, to a lesser extent, married couples became more mobile and generally succeeded in reallocating more of their total spending to discretionary areas. The propensity of retirees to purchase leisure more than doubled during the study period. For an additional dollar of 1987 income, 14 cents was allocated to leisure as measured by the sum of MPCs for food away from home, public transportation, other vehicle expenses, and entertainment. These findings provide important empirical evidence of the trend toward a more active retiree lifestyle, which has been discussed but not previously so clearly quantified in the literature. This changed retiree lifestyle has generally been assumed by business, but our research gives a much clearer image of the size and scope of this change. There are several possible explanations for this increased proclivity to spend on leisure. Since the prices of food and transportation increased at about the same rate as the overall CPI, the price effect is minimal. The 18 percent decline in the real price of entertainment may have been a motivating factor (U.S. Bureau of the Census, 1989). However, it appears that retiree preferences for leisure activities increased and they chose to spend a larger share of discretionary income on leisure. Better health, increased advertising, and enhanced leisure opportunities targeted at the retired probably contributed to this shift in preferences.

Housing expenditure has a unique role in retiree spending on necessities, compared with food and apparel. While all three retiree household types reallocated lesser budget shares to the necessity areas of food and apparel, the pattern for housing was more varied: single females continued to budget well over 40 percent on housing; single males reduced their housing share to less than 30 percent, which is now comparable to that for married couples. Since single elderly women constitute one of the most rapidly growing demographic groups, these findings highlight their often dire need for affordable housing.

Cash gifts and contributions is a particularly important category in analyzing retiree expenditure decisions, and this MPC declined substantially from 1972 to 1987. The reduction in the highest marginal tax rates, which increased the real cost of giving, is the most likely explanation. In addition, decreased financial assets, increased home ownership with illiquid equity, and increased life expectancy, which may have reduced the predisposition to disperse assets, may all be relevant factors.

We find that the retired significantly shifted their spending patterns. Their proclivity to purchase leisure items and health care increased, while their inclination to buy necessities and to make charitable contributions declined. Over time their overall APC has increased greatly, from 90 percent to 103 percent, signalling a major shift from positive net saving to dissaving. A very serious problem may develop if elderly persons continue to dissave at unsustainable rates. We also find that retirees' desire to spend declines with age (particularly in the 1987 period). This highlights the differences among retiree subgroups and the need to disaggregate retiree expenditure patterns by age, as well as by household type. Retirees are not a homogeneous group for the purposes of expenditure analysis. Our finding of a declining APC is not consistent with the Life Cycle Hypothesis, which posits that households tend to dissave more as they get older. This apparent contradiction of the Life Cycle Hypothesis may be due to concerns about increased longevity and rising health care costs, leading the retired to become more cautious about spending in the latter stages of the life cycle.

This chapter examined change in a broad array of expenditures by retirees over time. The following chapters analyze these expenditures in more detail. Chapter 4 examines the impact of entry into retirement on expenditure patterns and compares the expenditures of retired and nonretired households. Chapter 5 examines spending on necessities, focusing on the poor elderly and the impact of financial assistance on their expenditures. Chapter 6 explores the factors impacting health care expenditures in the 1980–1990 period.

APPENDIX

Econometric Methodology

The model for each of the CE expenditure categories is:

1. $C_i = \alpha_1 + \beta_1 I_i + \beta_2 \text{Age} (60–64)_i + \beta_3 \text{Age} (65–74)_i$
$+ \beta_4 \text{Age} (75+)_i + \beta_5 \text{Couple}_i + \beta_6 \text{SM}_i + \beta_7 \text{Race}_i$
$+ \beta_8 \text{High School}_i + \beta_9 \text{College}_i + \beta_{10} \text{College+}_i$
$+ \beta_{11} \text{Assets}_i + \varepsilon_i$

where

C_i = annual expenditures for household i

I_i = permanent income for household i

Couple$_i$ = 1 if household i is a married couple; 0 otherwise

SM_i = 1 if household is a single male; 0 otherwise

Race$_i$ = 1 if non-black; 0 otherwise

High school$_i$ = 1 if reference person i has high school education; 0 otherwise

College$_i$ = 1 if reference person i has college education; 0 otherwise

College+$_i$ = 1 if reference person i has graduate schooling; 0 otherwise

Age (60–64)$_i$ = 1 if reference person of household i is 60–64; 0 otherwise

Age (65–74)$_i$ = 1 if reference person of household i is 65–74; 0 otherwise

Age (75+)$_i$ = 1 if reference person of household i is 75+; 0 otherwise

Assets$_i$ = net asset value of household i

ε_i is the disturbance term.

Four econometric problems were addressed to estimate the expenditure equations. First, to solve a limited dependent variable problem we used a Tobit procedure because expenditures in some categories are zero. Second, a simultaneous equations Tobit procedure (Smith and Blundell, 1986) is used to solve an errors in variables problem, which arose because permanent income is not observable.

The model for the simultaneous Tobit regression is specified as follows:

2. $y_1^* = \beta_1'x_1 + \gamma y_2 + \varepsilon_1$ (Tobit)

3. $y_2 = \pi_2'x_2 + \varepsilon_2$

Equation 2 is a modified version of equation 1, where y_2 is observed total expenditure and x_1 is a matrix containing the other explanatory variables (household type dummies, age dummies, race dummy, education dummies, and assets) in equation 1. Total expenditures are estimated in equation 3 as a function of x_2, where x_2 includes observed income and all of the variables in x_1. Simultaneous equations bias is tested using Smith and Blundell's (1986) procedure.

Third, if the spending patterns of 1972 retirees differ from those of the 1987 retirees, structural change in the expenditure function should be observed. If the marginal propensity to consume (and the other coefficients) of these two time periods differ, a likelihood ratio test (a Chow [1960] type test) will reveal this. We test the null hypothesis that the regression coefficients in the expenditure equations for 1972 (β_{1972}) and 1987 (β_{1987}) are identical. The following test statistic has a χ^2 distribution with 12 degrees of freedom:

$$-2[\log L(\beta_{\text{full sample}}) - \log L(\beta_{1972}) - \log L(\beta_{1987})]$$

Fourth, the marginal effects in a Tobit model differ from those in a standard regression equation. We present both the estimated regression coefficients, β, (the partial derivatives of the expected value of the latent variable, $E[y^*|x]$, with respect to x, using the mean value of x), and Φ (the cumulative distribution function of the standard normal evaluated at ($\beta'x/\sigma$)). Note that Φ times β equals the partial derivative of $E[y|x]$ with respect to x,

4. $$\frac{\partial E[y|x]}{\partial x} = \Phi \beta$$

This partial derivative indicates the change in y (the observed expenditure) with respect to a change in x. An income elasticity can be formulated using this income derivative and $E[y|x]$ evaluated at the mean value of x using equation 6.37 in Maddala (1983).

NOTES

1. This chapter is based on Michael Nieswiadomy and Rose M. Rubin, 1995, Changes in expenditure patterns of retirees: 1972–73 and 1986–87, *Journal of Gerontology: Social Sciences*, 50B(5): S274–S290.

2. The 1972–1973 CE Interview Survey of 20,000 families, representative of the U.S. population, presents annual data. In the early 1980s, the CE Survey was changed from decennial collection of data to an annual ongoing interview (Gieseman, 1987).

3. These inflation adjustments are based on 1987 CPI = 340.4, 1972 CPI = 125.3, and 1973 CPI = 133.1.

4. We use the common acronym "MPC," even though it means marginal propensity to consume, rather than "MPS," because "MPS" usually refers to the marginal propensity to save.

5. We can infer that the quantity of apparel purchased increased for all three household types using the differential %ΔTR = %ΔQ + %ΔP, where TR is total revenue, Q is quantity, and P is price. For example, since apparel prices fell 35 percent and married couples spent 20 percent less on apparel, their quantity purchased increased by 15 percent.

6. The models for vehicles, reading, and education could not be estimated due to the large number of zero expenditures.

7. The detailed regression results for all of the models are reported in M. Nieswiadomy and R. M. Rubin, 1995, Changes in expenditure patterns of retirees: 1972–73 and 1986–87, *Journal of Gerontology: Social Sciences*, 50B(5): S274–S290.

8. Other vehicle expenses include vehicle finance charges, maintenance and repairs, vehicle insurance, vehicle rental, licenses, and other charges.

Chapter 4

The Effect of Retirement on Expenditures

Information on expenditure patterns on entry into and during retirement is important for both individual decision making and national policy planning. However, few studies have examined the manner in which the elderly manage their expenditures or how consumption patterns differ between the retired and the nonretired. The influence of retirement on expenditure patterns as well as on income sources, savings, and taxes of retired elderly households is examined in this chapter. The broad issues addressed are: How does entry into retirement impact expenditure patterns and income for different types of elderly households? How do expenditure patterns and income differ between retired and nonretired households?

To analyze these two questions, we use two separate but related studies. The first is an analysis of changes in the economic status of married couples, single males, and single females, over age 50, who retired during the survey year. Part of this analysis appeared in the *Journal of Applied Gerontology* (Rubin and Nieswiadomy, 1995). Changes in consumption patterns between the periods preceding and following retirement are compared by major expenditure categories and by detailed analysis of specific key categories such as health care, leisure activities, and travel. The second part of the analysis compares the economic status of retired and working households over the age of 50. Part of this analysis appeared in the *Monthly*

Labor Review (Rubin and Nieswiadomy, 1994). Expenditure shares for the same three household types were analyzed by age group and by income level to account for the heterogeneity of older Americans.

ENTRY INTO RETIREMENT

Entry into retirement can be both exciting and challenging for households as the realm of everyday life changes substantially with adjustments to a new lifestyle. Income and expenditure shifts are part of this adjustment. In this section we analyze the immediate changes that occur during the first year following retirement.[1]

Summary Statistics

A sample of 117 households entering retirement during 1984–1987 was drawn from the Consumer Expenditure Survey. The sample is disaggregated by household type into married couples, single males, and single females. Married couples comprise 66 percent of the sample. The category with the largest proportion of non-whites is single females at 22 percent. Single females tend to be better educated than single males, but among married couples, males received more education. A majority of respondents in each category worked at least 10 hours per week before retirement and most worked more than 35 hours. However, more than 75 percent of females in married couples were not working outside the home before the household's entry into retirement. At retirement, only single males showed any significant change in housing, with a 6 percent decline in renters and a corresponding 6 percent increase in those living in a home without a mortgage. Slightly over two-thirds of married couples lived in homes without mortgages, before and after retirement. Single females had the highest percentage of renters, 44 percent.

Income and selected financial assets before and after retirement are presented in Table 4.1 for each household type. The households in the sample reported multiple sources of income, ranging from 5 for single males to 13 for single females. The average after-tax income for the entire sample entering retirement was $19,340, which fell to $15,702 after retirement (constant 1987 dollars). While married couples experienced the largest monetary decline in income ($4,767 or 22 percent), single males actually experienced a slight increase. Single females, with the lowest after-tax incomes both before and after retirement, had a 25 percent decline due to retirement.

In comparing incomes of households of different sizes, it is appropriate to make an equivalence scale adjustment. Hurd (1990) recommends using

Table 4.1
Income and Assets of Households Entering Retirement
(1987 Dollars)

Income by source	Married Percent Share		Single Male Percent Share		Single Female Percent Share	
	Before	After	Before	After	Before	After
Wage & salary	32.8	0.0	39.7	0.0	55.5	0.0
Non-farm business	4.2	0.0	3.0	0.0	0.5	0.0
Social security & RRR	28.1	45.8	19.5	27.7	23.1	46.3
SSI	0.1	0.1	0.0	0.0	0.2	1.1
Dividends, royalties	5.7	11.9	3.0	9.6	3.2	9.0
Interest	10.3	12.9	13.6	30.7	1.6	11.4
Pensions & annuities	13.2	27.1	18.9	31.3	18.8	19.2
Welfare	0.0	0.0	0.0	0.0	0.3	0.5
Other	5.5	2.1	2.3	0.8	(3.2)	12.3
Income before tax	$23,660	$18,546	$18,537	$16,778	$14,425	$8,678
Income after tax	$22,050	$17,283	$15,208	$16,267	$13,318	$9,990
Selected assets						
Checking accounts	10.4	10.5	38.2	25.4	4.8	5.6
Savings accounts	55.9	51.3	45.1	56.8	45.7	62.1
Stocks and bonds	26.3	31.7	12.6	13.9	49.2	36.9
U.S. Govt. bonds	0.4	0.2	2.0	2.6	0.0	0.0
Money owed to CU	10.2	12.3	3.2	4.2	0.6	5.4
Debt	(3.2)	(6.0)	(1.2)	(2.8)	(0.4)	(10.1)
Net Selected Assets	$31,751	$31,155	$35,974	$28,253	$11,862	$8,735

Source: R. M. Rubin and M. Nieswiadomy, 1995, Economic adjustments of households on entry into retirement, *Journal of Applied Gerontology*, 14(4): 467–482. Reprinted by permission of Sage Publications, Inc.

a 37 percent adjustment for the second person, based on van der Gaag and Smolensky's (1982) study. In other words, a couple is deemed as well-off as a single person if their income is 37 percent higher. Based on this adjustment, before retirement married couples have higher adjusted after-tax income than single males, and single males have higher income than single females. After retirement, married couples have lower adjusted income after tax than single males, but higher than single females.

A number of the sample households received Social Security in conjunction with part-time work prior to designating themselves as retired. The amount received ranged from 63 to 87 percent of the after-retirement amount. For the entire sample of households entering retirement, Social Security (SS) and Railroad Retirement (RRR) (referred to jointly as SS for Social Security throughout the chapter) accounted for 26 percent of income before retirement, and 43 percent of income after retirement, with 86 percent of the households receiving SS after retirement. As expected, SS became a more important source of income after retirement. For married couples, this source provided 46 percent of income; SS also provided 46 percent of after-retirement income for single females, with 83 percent receiving some type of benefit. SS was a less important source of income for single males, providing only 28 percent of income with only 77 percent receiving it. For the entire sample, pensions and annuities were the next most important source of income after entering retirement (27 percent), followed by interest (15 percent). However, for single males, 47 percent received pensions and annuities, the most important source of income, which provided 31 percent of after-retirement income for the group. Also, 53 percent of single males received interest income, and it provided 31 percent of after retirement income (compared with 28 percent from SS). Only 30 percent of single females received pensions and annuities, which provided 19 percent of after-retirement income. Interest provided another 11 percent of their after-retirement income, with only 30 percent receiving it.

Preretirement mean wage and salary income for single females represented a slightly higher share than that for single males, but women's postretirement total income was only approximately half that of single males. Single females are the least financially secure group among the elderly, largely due to their much lower interest and pension components, not their Social Security payments, which were only $553 lower annually.

Total tax payments and all specific taxes declined following retirement for all of the household categories, with the largest decrease occurring for single males. Single females have a negative income tax (–$1,312) after retirement, with negative taxes of each type except for very low personal property taxes.

Expenditures

Average annualized expenditures, shown in Table 4.2, were classified into 14 categories (including a specially created category for trips). All households decreased their total expenditures after retirement by 12 percent, while their after-tax incomes decreased a little more than 19 percent. These declines were quite unevenly distributed among the family types. Married households who dissaved a few hundred dollars before retirement, subsequently dissaved several thousand after retirement, primarily because their after-tax incomes declined by 22 percent. Similarly, the average total expenditures of single females declined only slightly in the face of a one-quarter decrease in after-tax income, causing their postretirement dissaving to be as high as 15 percent of after-tax income. In contrast, for single

Table 4.2
Average Annual Expenditure Shares of Households Entering Retirement (1987 Dollars)

	Married		Single Male		Single Female	
	Percent Share		Percent Share		Percent Share	
	Before	After	Before	After	Before	After
Food	18.9	18.4	19.5	19.6	14.6 *	18.9
Alcoholic beverage	1.3	1.3	0.6 *	1.9	0.7	0.5
Housing	32.7	33.0	38.2	34.9	51.7 *	45.5
Apparel and services	3.7	3.8	3.3	2.9	3.6	3.2
Transportation	15.8	15.9	21.2 *	13.7	9.3	10.3
Health care	10.9 *	13.2	6.1 *	9.8	8.1	9.2
Entertainment	5.4 *	3.9	3.7	4.4	3.5	3.2
Personal care	1.7 *	1.5	0.8	2.0	1.8	1.8
Reading & Education	1.0	0.9	1.0	1.5	1.2	0.9
Tobacco	1.8 *	1.4	1.8	2.5	1.3	1.1
Miscellaneous	1.2	1.9	1.3	3.7	1.1	1.1
Cash gifts & contributions	4.0	2.5	1.5	1.9	2.6	3.5
Insurance & pension	1.6 *	2.5	1.2	1.2	0.8	1.0
Trips	3.1	5.3	2.3	4.2	0.9	1.5
Total average expenditures	$22,368	$20,412	$17,441	$9,622	$11,527	$11,446

*Before and after shares are statistically different at p<0.10.

Source: R. M. Rubin and M. Nieswiadomy, 1995, Economic adjustments of households on entry into retirement, *Journal of Applied Gerontology*, 14(4): 467–482. Reprinted by permission of Sage Publications, Inc.

males, less than 60 percent of after-tax income was spent on consumption in the period following retirement.

All of the household groups exhibit approximately the expected ranges of budget shares. Differences in mean budget shares before and after entry into retirement were analyzed with share t-tests. While household mean dollar expenditures decreased for all households (with single females having only very slight declines), most of their expenditure shares do not change significantly. The disaggregated groups reveal only ten significant (p<0.10) expenditure share changes. However, the significant changes vary substantially among the three types of households.

For married couple households, health care and life insurance expenditure shares increased, while their entertainment, personal care, and tobacco shares declined. For single males, the expenditure shares for alcohol and health care increased, while the transportation share decreased. In contrast, for single females, the food expenditure share increased, while housing decreased significantly.

Expenditure Regression Results

Many factors affect consumer demand for goods and services, including income, age, marital status, race, gender, education, and assets. A multiple regression model is generally the most appropriate method to analyze the various effects of these factors, as regression analysis enables us to determine the partial effect of each variable, ceteris paribus. However, the simplest type of regression analysis, ordinary least squares (OLS), is not appropriate in our analysis because some of the expenditures for some categories are zero for some households. To correctly estimate these expenditure equations, we use Tobit regression analysis, as described in the appendix to Chapter 3.

Tobit regression models were run on household CE Survey expenditure categories for the same households before and after retirement. The impacts of three continuous independent variables (age, assets, and total expenditure, which is a proxy for permanent income) and family type, race, and education level on expenditures were analyzed. The base case is a single female, non-white, with eight years or less of education.

The marginal propensities to consume (MPCs) for the expenditure regressions are presented in Table 4.3. The method for calculating MPCs in a Tobit model is discussed in the appendix to Chapter 3. The Chow tests, measuring whether the coefficients before retirement differ from those after retirement, reveal several areas of significant difference: food, apparel, household operations, transportation (and gas, other vehicles, and public

Table 4.3
Tobit Regression Estimates of the Marginal Propensity to Consume (MPC) Before and After Retirement

Category	Before	After	Category	Before	After
Food	0.070 *	0.058 *	Health care	0.044 *	0.148 *
Food at home	0.010	0.023 *	Health insurance	0.030 *	0.006
Food away	0.003	0.029 *	Medical services	0.004	0.094 *
			Prescription drugs	0.004	0.007 *
Alcoholic beverage	0.004 *	0.011 *			
			Entertainment	0.008	0.056 *
Housing	0.081 *	0.180 *	Fees & admissions	0.005 *	0.058 *
Shelter	0.038 *	0.100 *	TVs & radios	0.002	0.002
Owned dwelling	0.020 *	0.045 *	Other equipment	0.002 *	0.001
Rented dwelling	0.001	-0.008			
Other dwelling	0.009 *	0.013 *	Personal care	0.002 *	0.006 *
Utilities & services	0.013 *	0.025 *			
House operations	0.004 *	0.012 *	Tobacco	-0.002	0.002
House furnishing	0.018 *	0.024 *			
			Miscellaneous	0.002	0.008
Apparel & services	0.007 *	0.022 *			
			Gifts & contributions	0.145 *	0.028 *
Transportation	0.269 *	0.277 *			
Gasoline & oil	0.014 *	0.030 *	Insurance	0.001	0.010 *
Other vehicle	0.002 *	0.049 *			
Public transport.	-0.002	0.013 *	Trips	0.020 *	0.080 *

*Statistically significant at $p<0.10$.

Source: R. M. Rubin and M. Nieswiadomy, 1995, Economic adjustments of households on entry into retirement, *Journal of Applied Gerontology*, 14(4): 467–482. Reprinted by permission of Sage Publications, Inc.

transportation), health (and medical services), entertainment (and subcategories of fees and admissions, TVs, radios, and other equipment), cash gifts and contributions, and life insurance.[2]

Comparisons of the MPCs indicate some important changes in consumer purchases immediately after retirement. Among the statistically significant MPCs, only three categories (food, health insurance, and cash gifts and contributions) have larger MPCs before entry into retirement, but the MPCs for 23 categories are larger after retirement. Among the most interesting shifts in household MPCs are the substantial increases for items related to leisure (entertainment, public transportation, fees and admissions, food away from home, and trips) and for medical services. Gifts and contributions shows a notable decline in MPC. These relative shifts in the postretirement MPCs reflect a reallocation from work-related costs to health and leisure activities. The importance of income as an explanatory variable increased after entry into retirement. Increased availability of leisure time appears to allow households to utilize income differently than before retirement.

Based on these MPCs, we calculated expenditure elasticities for each consumption item before and after retirement. The only item with a preretirement elasticity greater than one is cash gifts. After retirement, several items appear to be luxuries: alcohol, other dwellings, transportation (and public transportation), health care (and medical services), fees and admissions, and trips. The large increase in the MPC for health care (in Table 4.4, the Tobit coefficient on permanent income increases from 0.05 to 0.21)[3] may be due to the loss of work-related health insurance, or due to changes in health status that affected the decision to retire. The trips permanent income coefficient also increased sharply after retirement (in Table 4.4, the Tobit coefficient on permanent income increases from 0.08 to 0.27).[4] In sum, these elasticities reveal the preference of the newly retired for increased spending on alcohol, trips, public transportation, and fees and admissions, reflecting utilization of their new leisure time.

We also estimated the sociodemographic effects of age, race, education, and family type on expenditures. Four of these Tobit regressions (food away from home, owned dwelling, health care, and trips) are shown in Table 4.4, but we discuss results of some additional models. Prior to retirement, age has positive effects on gifts and health care spending and negative impacts on alcohol, owned dwelling, other dwelling, apparel, tobacco, transportation, and other entertainment equipment spending. The overall effect of age, after retirement, is negative for all categories except health care and gifts and contributions. Race has some effect on consumption decisions of those entering retirement. After retirement, whites spend more than non-whites on food, food away from home, gas and oil, and other vehicle expenses, ceteris paribus.

After retirement single males spend less on food at home, health insurance, and cash gifts and more on gas and tobacco. This lower expenditure on health insurance by single males vis-à-vis single females is consistent with Smeeding and Straub's (1987) finding that the households least able to afford it are likely to pay more out of pocket for health insurance.

Assets affected very few categories, with a negative effect on life insurance purchases before retirement. After retirement, assets had a negative

Table 4.4
Selected Tobit Expenditure Regressions Before and After Retirement

	Food away from home		Owned Dwelling		Health Care		Trips	
	Before	After	Before	After	Before	After	Before	After
Constant	-1081.40	-1829.90 *	1470.10	-725.65	-4599.60 *	-7630.60 *	-3518.20	-6357.50
Permanent Income	0.01	0.04 *	0.04 *	0.07 *	0.05 *	0.21 *	0.08 *	0.27 *
Elasticity	0.14	0.72	0.19	0.44	0.50	0.92	0.42	1.11
Age	-4.91	7.28	-72.05 *	-45.66	68.42 *	81.19 *	-77.05	-87.97
Couple	514.47 *	257.24	1302.40	302.39	538.01 *	-417.95	2574.10 *	2336.90
Single Male	270.19	381.60	237.20	37.68	-589.74	-953.86	59.90	3109.00
Race (white)	739.64 *	597.92 *	1367.20	1721.00	-13.68	1104.20	191.17	319.95
Education(High School)	741.19 *	289.30 *	1629.20 *	1675.90 *	544.95 *	543.17	3112.30 *	2508.80
Education(College)	758.94 *	494.31 *	463.74	1412.50	138.81	-567.46	3762.90 *	5592.80 *
Education(College+)	902.85 *	-456.47	5392.30 *	3788.10 *	-124.30	524.22	1620.00	-2802.40
Assets ($1000)	1.20	0.40	5.00	10.00 *	1.60	-1.50	7.50	18.50
R2	0.10	0.14	0.06	0.08	0.17	0.09	0.05	0.10
Log-Likelihood	-134.53	-141.20	-228.38	-217.98	-184.55	-292.10	-158.12	-177.66
Chow Test	15.18		5.08		145.46 *		13.02	
Φ	0.65	0.67	0.58	0.60	0.87	0.70	0.27	0.30
Limit Observations	31.00	28.00	84.00	81.00	8.00	8.00	75.00	71.00
LR test	28.94 *	44.30 *	30.16 *	37.98 *	73.70 *	57.54 *	16.76 *	38.06 *

*Statistically significant at p<0.10.

Source: M. Nieswiadomy and R. M. Rubin, 1991, Changes in household economic status upon entry into retirement, Paper presented at 66th Annual Conference of the Western Economic Association International, Seattle, July 1, 1991.

impact on transportation and tobacco spending and a positive impact on shelter, other dwellings, entertainment, and gifts and contributions. The largest assets coefficient is for the gifts model after retirement, indicating that one cent of each additional asset dollar is spent on gifts.

Marital status is a less influential determinant of expenditures, as married couples spend differently than single females in over two-thirds of the expenditure categories before retirement; however, after retirement, married couples spend differently than single females in only about one half of the categories.

Educational status tends to have a positive effect on expenditures. While education level affects about half of the expenditure categories prior to retirement, the impact is much more limited after retirement. However, college-educated households spend significantly more ($5,593) on trips than less-than-high-school-educated households in 1987.

RETIRED VERSUS NONRETIRED

The previous section highlighted some of the short-term adjustments made by households as they enter retirement. Because numerous other adjustments occur over the years of the retirement phase, comparison of the expenditure patterns of retired and nonretired households contributes to further understanding these adjustments. In this section we examine the factors that affect the expenditure functions of retired and nonretired households.[5]

Summary Statistics

The study sample includes 2,607 households age 50 and over from the 1986 and 1987 CE fifth interview surveys. The fifth interview was used because it is the only interview in which the household records asset information. All retired household types had lower average incomes than their working counterparts, but the income difference was smaller for couples than for singles. Mean after-tax income of retired couples is 58 percent of the income of nonretired couples, compared to 53 percent for single females, and only 48 percent for single males. Even after adjusting for household size using van der Gaag and Smolensky's (1982) equivalence scale, retired and nonretired married couples are better off than single men or women. After-tax income of retired single males is 44 percent less, and the after-tax income of single females is 55 percent less than that of married couples. Each of the three groups displays considerably higher educational attainment for the nonretired than for the retired. Home ownership varies among the three groups, with single males having the lowest ownership status and couples the highest; nearly half of all single males age 50 and over are renters.

Income and Assets

Analysis of income, taxes, and assets of retired and nonretired couples and single male and female households by age category shows some distinct patterns, as shown in Table 4.5.[6] In general, for each of the three types

Table 4.5
Income and Asset Shares of Retired and Nonretired Households (1987 Dollars)

	Married		Single Male		Single Female	
	Retired	Nonret.	Retired	Nonret.	Retired	Nonret.
Income by source	n=692	n=622	n=218	n=141	n=687	n=247
Wage & salary	10.0	67.4	0.0	72.9	0.0	70.2
Non-farm business	0.5	10.4	0.0	6.5	0.0	5.2
Social security & RRR	43.2	7.2	46.2	5.8	57.7	9.5
SSI	0.4	0.0	1.9	0.0	1.4	0.1
Dividends, royalties	7.1	2.2	8.6	1.3	8.1	2.3
Interest	12.2	4.9	16.1	5.1	10.2	5.4
Pensions & annuities	23.7	6.5	23.1	6.6	16.8	4.0
Welfare	0.1	0.0	0.4	0.1	0.2	0.1
Workmen's comp.	1.0	0.1	2.3	0.5	1.3	0.3
Other	1.6	1.3	1.4	1.2	4.2	3.0
Income before tax	$19,462	$36,090	$11,241	$23,620	$8,665	$17,614
Income after tax	$18,373	$31,894	$10,142	$21,272	$8,363	$15,679
Value of selected assets						
Checking accounts	11.3	11.5	18.0	21.5	10.7	10.6
Savings accounts	56.9	49.3	57.3	40.1	56.2	42.8
Stocks and bonds	28.7	36.8	23.1	37.1	31.1	42.3
U.S. Govt. bonds	3.1	2.3	1.5	1.3	2.0	4.2
Total Selected Assets	$27,505	$28,407	$18,229	$24,039	$11,129	$15,750

Source: R. M. Rubin and M. Nieswiadomy, 1994, Expenditure patterns of retired and nonretired persons, *Monthly Labor Review*, 117(4): 10–21.

of households, average income declines with age. Although after-tax income declines for both retired and nonretired married couple households after age 60, assets decline with increasing age for the retired but increase with age for the nonretired. For retired couples, financial assets of the younger, age 50 to 59 group are less than half those of the other age groups. For the oldest retirees (85+), both after-tax income and financial assets are about one-fifth lower than for the other age groups. After age 65, Social Security becomes the primary income source, with interest and pensions and annuities being second and third.

Retired single males age 50 to 59 appear to be relatively well off, having incomes and assets that exceed those of the couples in the same age group. They have a variety of relatively high income sources, which may explain their early retirement status. In contrast, the incomes of the other single male retirees are quite low, and their primary source of income is Social Security. The overall financial picture for retired single women appears bleak. For those under age 60, pensions and annuities account for almost half of their meager income, and after-tax income is larger than pretax, due to tax subsidies. Further, this group has negligible financial assets. Once eligibility age is reached, Social Security is the mainstay of all retired single women and of those nonretired over age 75. For retired women receiving Social Security, average after-tax income remains close to the "near poverty" level of $7,128.

Expenditures

Overall, we find that nonretired households spend more than the comparable retired group: married couples spend 45 percent more, single males spend 65 percent more, and single females spend 50 percent more (see Table 4.6). Compared with retired single women, married couples spend 87 percent more, and single males spend 21 percent more.

Table 4.6 also reveals that almost all expenditure shares differed significantly when comparing the total retired sample with the nonretired. The nonretired allocated a greater share to food away from home, alcoholic beverages, owned and other dwellings, home furnishings, apparel and services, all transportation except public, entertainment, education, miscellaneous, gifts, and insurance. In contrast, retired households spent a significantly greater share on food, food at home, housing, rented dwellings, utilities, household operations, and health care, according to the share t-tests.

All three retired groups spend a significantly greater share of their total expenditures than the nonretired on food at home, utilities, and health care.

Table 4.6
Average Annual Expenditure Shares of Retired and Nonretired Households (Age 50+)

	All Households		Married		Single Male		Single Female	
	Retired	Nonret.	Retired	Nonret.	Retired	Nonret.	Retired	Nonret.
Food	20.3 *	17.7	21.1 *	18.2	21.2 *	18.2	19.4 *	16.4
Alcoholic beverage	0.9 *	1.5	1.1 *	1.4	2.0	2.7	0.4 *	1.0
Housing	38.0 *	34.3	32.0	31.4	36.5	36.7	44.6 *	40.5
Apparel and services	3.4 *	4.8	3.6 *	4.8	2.7	3.3	3.4 *	5.7
Transportation	10.6 *	16.2	13.5 *	17.1	14.5	16.0	6.9 *	13.9
Health care	12.6 *	7.4	13.2 *	8.5	9.7 *	5.5	12.8 *	6.1
Entertainment	2.9 *	4.5	3.5 *	4.6	2.5 *	4.1	2.4 *	4.4
Personal care	1.4	1.3	1.5	1.4	0.8	0.7	1.6	1.7
Reading & Education	1.1	1.2	1.0	1.2	1.0	1.0	1.0	1.1
Tobacco	1.4	1.5	1.5	1.5	2.1	1.7	1.0 *	1.6
Miscellaneous	1.6 *	2.2	1.5 *	2.2	2.0	3.4	1.7	2.0
Cash gifts & contributions	4.2 *	5.1	4.9	5.4	3.6	5.0	3.8	4.4
Life & personal insurance	1.3 *	2.2	1.7 *	2.5	1.3	1.9	1.1	1.5
Total average expenditure	$13,180	$21,648	$17,540	$25,340	$11,340	$18,652	$9,368	$14,048

Note: Total average expenditures do not include contributions to pensions and social security.
*Shares for retired and nonretired are statistically different at a p<0.10 level.

Source: R. M. Rubin and M. Nieswiadomy, 1994, Expenditure patterns of retired and nonretired persons, *Monthly Labor Review,* 117(4): 10–21.

Retired couples and single females also spend a significantly greater share on food and rented dwellings, while retired single men spend a significantly greater share on entertainment and retired single females spend more on household operations.

Expenditures of the Retired by Age. We examined the expenditures of the retired group in more detail, first by age groups and then by income levels. From age 50 to age 84, aggregate spending encompassed by the three major areas of food, housing, and transportation consistently declines from 71 percent to 64 percent of total spending, but these categories comprise 68 percent of expenditures for those 85 and over. Expenditure patterns appear to change substantially for this oldest age group; the share of food in their budgets increases, while transportation declines dramatically. This is consistent with the perception that they are likely to give up cars at this stage and to generally incur reduced mobility. The 50 to 59 age group differs from the age 60 to 84 groups, in particular, spending a greater share on housing. Both of the extreme retiree age groups allocate a considerably smaller share to cash gifts and contributions than those between age 60 and 84. Overall, there is a steady increase with age in the combined share spent on utilities and household operations (increasing by 7 percent), and also in the share spent on health care, which increases steeply after age 65.

Average annual expenditures of single male retirees remain less than $10,000 up to age 65, increase for the next two age groups, and then decline precipitously for those age 85 and over. Among those age 85 and over, the share spent on health care by single males was more than twice as large as that of single females, and 59 percent larger than that of married couples. For retired single females, total average expenditures change very little from age 50 to 85, but their aggregate spending for the three areas of food, housing, and transportation declines from 78 percent to 67 percent. Retired women age 85 and over devote 51 percent of their expenditures to housing. The spending shares for health care and for gifts and contributions follow the same patterns for single females as for married couples. Health care expenditure shares for single women increase substantially with age, and especially for those over age 65. For all three household types, gifts and contributions are much higher between the ages of 60 and 84.

Expenditures of the Retired by Income Group. We also analyzed expenditures of retired households by income levels. Four income categories were selected on the basis of the 1986 federal poverty level thresholds and the three after-tax income categories delineated by Moehrle (1990), as shown in Table 3.4.[7] In this study, we utilize the poverty levels for the nonaged because our sample includes persons over age 50 and the poverty lines for the aged apply only to those age 65 and over.

There are fewer single males and almost three times as many single females below the single-person poverty level as couples below the two-person poverty level. We find only about 16 percent of single males and 9 percent of single females having incomes greater than $15,000, in contrast to almost 48 percent of married couples. Overall, the majority of the total sample has income between their group poverty level and $15,000.

Single male retirees with poverty level incomes spend high shares on food (25 percent) and housing (37 percent). Single females below the poverty level spend a much smaller share on food and a larger share on housing than single males. The total share committed to these two necessity categories equals approximately 60 percent for both groups. In contrast, couples below the poverty level spend only about 46 percent on these two basic areas. As income increases, all three family groups devote a larger share of their expenditures to gifts and contributions, with the amount exceeding $3,000 for each group, and ranging from an 11 to 15 percent share of expenditures for those with incomes greater than $30,000.

For married couples above the poverty level, the shares of total expenditure allocated to food, food at home, housing, and health care decline as income increases. For all married couples, the shares of spending on food away from home, apparel and services, transportation, and entertainment increase as income increases.

Savings

Savings is measured by subtracting total expenditures (Table 4.6) from after-tax income (Table 4.5). Among the retired, married couples aged 60 to 64, single males over the age of 64, and single females aged 50 to 84 dissave, that is, their expenditures exceed their after-tax income. Retiree income is 42 percent less for married couples than that for the nonretired, 52 percent less for single males, and 47 percent less for single females. A similar pattern is found in expenditures, with married couple households spending 31 percent less after retirement than those not retired, while single males spend 39 percent less, and single females spend 33 percent less. Both married couple and single female households appear to make fewer adjustments than single males following retirement when considering only percent changes in income and expenditures. However, single female households have lower absolute income and expenditures.

Comparing differences between income and expenditures by age level, retired married couples of all age groups (except 60 to 65) spend less than their after-tax income. Of the retired single male households, the younger age group, 50–59, spends slightly less than half of their after-tax income. This indicates a higher propensity to save than that of any other retired household age group. The three older age groups of retired single males dissave substantial amounts. Single females dissave at the beginning of retirement and through age 74; the age 85+ group has income that barely exceeds expenditures.

Expenditure Regression Results

As in the previous section, we estimate expenditure equations using Tobit regression analysis. The explanatory factors include income, age, marital status, race, gender, education, and assets. The only difference in this model is that age is measured using categorical (i.e., dummy) variables with the base case a 50–59 year old person. The dummy variables for age are 60–64, 65–74, and 75 and over. The expenditure categories for nonretired and retired households over age 50 were regressed on two continuous independent variables (financial assets and income) and dummy variables for family status, age group, race, and education level. The base case is a single black female, in age group 50–59, with eight years or less of education.

As in the previous section, we do not present the detailed regression results for all of the models. However, we present the MPCs for each expenditure category for the retired and nonretired in Table 4.7 and the coefficients and summary statistics for four selected expenditure regressions in Table 4.8. The Chow tests indicate that there is a significant difference between the coefficients in the retired and nonretired models for all of the expenditure categories. The likelihood ratio tests were statistically significant at the .01 level for all of the models, indicating that they explain the variation in the dependent variables. The methodology is described in the Appendix to Chapter 3.

MPCs and Expenditure Elasticities. The marginal propensity to spend (MPC) (labeled the permanent income coefficient) for each expenditure category is shown in Table 4.7. The nonretired have a higher MPC for housing, shelter, owned dwelling, other dwelling, and life insurance. The retired have a higher MPC for all categories of food, household furnishings, apparel, transportation, gas and motor oil, other vehicle expenses, public transportation, health care, entertainment, and cash gifts and contributions. Most notable is the higher MPC of the retired for transportation, indicating a greater desire to travel. The items with expenditure elasticities greater than one (luxury goods) for retired households shown in

Table 4.7
Tobit Regression Estimates of the Marginal Propensity to Consume (MPC): Retired and Nonretired Households

Category	Retired	Nonret.	Category	Retired	Nonret.
Food	0.138 *	0.099 *	Health care	0.044 *	-0.007
Food at home	0.056 *	0.038 *			
Food away	0.068 *	0.060 *	Entertainment	0.048 *	0.030 *
Alcoholic beverage	0.011 *	0.013 *	Reading	0.010 *	0.011 *
Housing	0.282 *	0.316 *	Personal care	0.012 *	0.008 *
Shelter	0.105 *	0.168 *			
Owned dwelling	0.055 *	0.114 *	Tobacco	0.000	-0.001
Rented dwelling	0.001	-0.013			
Other dwelling	0.009 *	0.031 *	Miscellaneous	0.040 *	0.026 *
Utilities & service	0.029 *	0.039 *			
House operations	0.019 *	0.022 *	Gifts/contributions	0.097 *	0.081 *
House furnishing	0.052 *	0.044 *			
			Life insurance	0.002 *	0.022 *
Apparel & services	0.065 *	0.058 *			
Transportation	0.214 *	0.158 *			
Gasoline & oil	0.012 *	0.008 *			
Other vehicle	0.061 *	0.039 *			
Public transport.	0.015 *	0.010 *			

*Statistically significant at $p<0.10$.

Source: R. M. Rubin and M. Nieswiadomy, 1994, Expenditure patterns of retired and nonretired persons, *Monthly Labor Review*, 117(4): 10–21.

Table 4.7 are: food away from home, alcohol, household furnishings and equipment, apparel, other vehicle expenses, and reading. The only luxury goods for the working households are other dwellings, household operations, and reading.

Specific Regressions. Food, owned dwelling, public transportation, and entertainment were selected for presentation of the detailed regression models to highlight significant contrasts in retired and nonretired consumption patterns. Spending on food and owned dwelling is representative

Table 4.8
Selected Tobit Expenditure Regressions of Households (Age 50+): Retired and Nonretired

	Food		Owned Dwelling		Public Transportation		Entertainment	
	Retired	Nonret	Retired	Nonret	Retired	Nonret	Retired	Nonret
Constant	269.48	10.76	-2281.00 *	-2315.30 *	-2545.90 *	-1281.40 *	-1884.20 *	-1170.50 *
Permanent Income	0.15 *	0.11 *	0.12 *	0.19 *	0.07 *	0.04 *	0.10 *	0.05 *
Elasticity	0.73	0.62	0.56	0.91	0.49	0.54	0.87	0.35
Married Couple	594.79 *	692.45 *	530.21 *	12.44	-687.71 *	-1058.40 *	7.15	292.79
Single Male	170.72	130.34	-974.10 *	-1916.60 *	-411.83	-230.36	-123.08	-336.85
Race (non-black)	7.67	385.76	642.89 *	286.33	-895.47 *	-818.50 *	595.11 *	477.15 *
Education (High School)	86.43	196.44	-4.15	-313.71	-28.12	-941.23 *	141.07	67.25
Education (College)	-90.12	-111.64	338.00	-246.25	14.60	-439.40	-30.92	349.75
Education (College+)	238.67	-306.65	880.40 *	-237.18	423.34	201.21	231.06	1124.10 *
Age (60-64)	-86.10	406.69	13.97	-614.55	243.22	155.22	86.09	-131.69
Age (65-74)	47.32	305.12	-507.83	-304.15	300.03	355.08	36.30	-372.65
Age (75+)	-246.61	386.10	724.48	-1394.30	193.66	-71.03	-276.60	-1192.40 *
Assets	-0.0041 *	0.0005	0.0004	0.0014	0.0062 *	0.0062 *	0.0021	0.0102 *
Likelihood Ratio Test	438.46 *	203.48 *	140.43 *	139.33 *	95.01 *	98.21 *	218.36 *	113.34 *
Log-Likelihood	-5349.01	-4173.33	-2760.87	-4372.44	-1495.96	-988.09	-5261.63	-2297.22
Chow Test		437.04 *		265.88 *		20.04 *		454.76 *
Φ	0.92	0.90	0.46	0.60	0.21	0.25	0.48	0.60
Limit Observations	6.00	0.00	751.00	344.00	1182.00	717.00	533.00	140.00

*Statistically significant at p<0.10.

Source: R. M. Rubin and M. Nieswiadomy, 1994, Expenditure patterns of retired and nonretired persons, *Monthly Labor Review,* 117(4): 10–21.

of a household's consumption of necessities, whereas public transportation and entertainment reflect leisure activities.

For spending on food, income is the only positive and significant explanatory variable for both groups, except that married couples spend more than single females. The retired have a larger income elasticity for food. The only other significant variable is assets, which has a negative effect on food expenditures for the retired. For owned dwelling, among the retired, single females spend $974 more than single males, but $530 less than couples. Among the nonretired, single females spend much more on owned dwelling ($1,916) than single males. For the retired, non-blacks spend more on owned dwellings ($642) and those with postcollege education spend more ($880) than eighth-grade-educated households.

Non-blacks, ceteris paribus, spend less on public transportation (–$895 and –$818 in Table 4.8) and more on entertainment ($595 and $477) for both retired and nonretired. In addition, the working higher-educated households spend more on entertainment ($1,124). The working group age 75 and over spends significantly less on entertainment (–$1,192) than the working age 50–59 group.

CONCLUSIONS

In this chapter, we examined the economic effects of a major life-cycle turning point. The findings provide insight into how the retirement lifestyle influences budget reallocations and how income changes affect consumption patterns. The findings also indicate the extent to which the elderly dissave to maintain their preretirement standard of living.

Retirement impacts the three types of households differently. Clearly, married couples fare better than single households following and during retirement. After adjustment for household size, couples' income is substantially larger than that of singles. Over twice as many single males and almost three times as many single females have incomes below poverty as do couples. Further, single females suffer the largest income decline, and this is not offset by concurrent expenditure decreases. They begin dissaving in the first quarter of retirement, and this continues throughout retirement. Only married couples do not dissave later in retirement.

The overall financial picture for retired single women appears bleak. Social Security is the mainstay of their income, as their pension income is low and their low level of financial assets generates little income. An additional concern for retired women is the large share of spending devoted to housing, primarily for utilities and household operations.

The retired spend a significantly greater share on food at home, utilities, household operations, and health care than the nonretired, and a smaller share on food away from home, alcohol, owned dwellings, furnishings, apparel, transportation, entertainment, gifts, and insurance. The shares spent on health care, utilities, and household operations increases with age. For retirees age 85 and over, both after-tax income and financial assets are about one-fifth lower than for younger retirees. As consumption overall declines, expenditure patterns change substantially for this age group; the share of food in their budgets increases, while transportation declines dramatically. The increase in purchase of health care upon retirement may indicate that retirement entry is often necessitated by ill health.

The regression analyses highlight some important behavioral changes on entry into retirement, particularly for expenditures on transportation, health, and entertainment. Once people are retired, the household's propensity to purchase health care, entertainment, and trips increases.

Interestingly, even though the retired have smaller budget shares for transportation, entertainment, and gifts, their MPCs are greater than those of the nonretired. These findings indicate that the retired have the desire to lead active lifestyles by traveling and entertaining if their incomes increase.

Retired households appear to be taking advantage of their retirement time with time-consuming entertainment and travel activities, as revealed in the high income elasticities ($\varepsilon > 1$, i.e., luxuries) of some key items. Immediately following retirement, several categories are luxuries: alcohol, transportation, medical services, fees and admissions, and trips. Later in retirement, food away from home, alcohol, household furnishings and equipment, apparel, other vehicle expenses, and reading are luxuries.

The single retired female appears to be more generous in giving gifts than married couples and single males. While retired single males spend significantly more on food away from home and transportation, they spend less on housing and shelter, utilities, household operations, house furnishings, apparel, and personal care than single females. All of these suggest that single females spend more time and income at home compared to single males.

Some demographic findings are interesting. Retired non-blacks spend more on health care and entertainment but less on gifts and contributions than comparable black households. Our findings confirm that spending on health care is positively correlated with education levels. This may be due to better recognition of the importance of health care or better insurance coverage for the higher-educated groups. Older age groups spend less on alcohol and more on health care.

Policy implications of these findings are quite significant. In light of increasing life spans, current workers need to start financial retirement planning early to avoid the dissaving problems of many current retirees. Retired single females dissave at unsustainable rates. Their income is less than half of that of married couples, even though on an equivalency basis a two-person household needs only about 37 percent more income to have the same standard of living. Furthermore, there is a need for low-income housing for many single females and for some single males, who are often renters.

Businesses are becoming more aware of retirees as a market force, and we provide empirical findings of the magnitude of the change in retiree propensities to spend, especially for entertainment and trips. After retirement, the proclivity to purchase trips quadruples, and spending also increases for food away from home and entertainment.

NOTES

1. This section is based on Rose M. Rubin and Michael Nieswiadomy, 1995, Economic adjustments of households on entry into retirement, *Journal of Applied Gerontology*, (14)4: 467–482.

2. Due to space constraints, the detailed results are not presented here. Only the MPCs for each model are presented in Table 3.3. Four of the models are shown in Table 3.4. The other detailed models are available from the authors upon request.

3. The MPC for health care before retirement was 0.044 (=0.05*0.87) and the MPC after retirement was 0.147 (=0.21*0.7). See the appendix to Chapter 3 for an explanation of the calculation of the MPC in a Tobit model.

4. The MPC for trips before retirement was 0.022 (=0.08*0.27) and the MPC after retirement was 0.081 (=0.27*0.3).

5. This section is based on Rose M. Rubin and Michael Nieswiadomy, 1994, Expenditure patterns of retired and non-retired persons, *Monthly Labor Review*, 117(4): 10–21.

6. Detailed unpublished tables stratified by age group are available from the authors upon request.

7. Detailed unpublished tables showing expenditure shares stratified by income groups are also available upon request from the authors. The poverty thresholds for the nonelderly in 1986 were $7,373 for two-person and $5,702 for one-person households, and for the elderly they were $6,630 and $4,255 respectively (Schulz, 1992).

Chapter 5

The Vulnerable Elderly

The economic well-being of older Americans is a central issue of numerous critical policy questions for the twenty-first century. These include reducing federal budget deficits; the financial viability of Social Security, Medicare, and other intergenerational transfers; and broader health care policies (Rubin and Koelln, 1996). The elderly have benefitted from a broader security net than the population as a whole, because of targeted programs including Social Security, Supplemental Security Income (SSI), Medicare, and means-tested programs such as Medicaid, food stamps, and subsidized housing. A limited but growing number of the elderly also receive Aid to Families with Dependent Children (AFDC). In an average month in 1990, 12 percent of the population aged 65 and over received major welfare assistance, compared with 8 percent of those aged 18 to 64. Further, elderly beneficiaries of assistance programs are more likely to be long-term participants than the nonelderly (U.S. Bureau of the Census, 1996c).

Historically, the income of older persons generally declined by a third to one-half after age 65, giving them the lowest income of any age group in the United States (Soldo, 1980). However, in more recent years important income changes have occurred for the elderly. While 35 percent of those age 65 and over had incomes below the poverty level as late as 1959,[1] this share declined to 10.5 percent in 1995. Despite rising average incomes, nearly 4 million older Americans remain below the poverty threshold of $141 per week for an elderly single person (U.S. Bureau of the Census, 1996a, 1996c).

Numerous researchers have examined specific expenditure areas and spending patterns of various groups, including groups of the elderly. However, only a limited number of analyses have expressly covered economically vulnerable older households. In a recent study, Meyer and Bartolomei-Hill (1994) found that elderly SSI recipients cannot afford a basic-needs package of housing, food, and medical care. They concluded that even though SSI benefits vary considerably across states, couples are generally better off than singles among elderly SSI recipients, and SSI benefits are substantially greater than AFDC benefits provided to elderly households. The literature suggests additional areas for analysis, and the objective of this chapter is to fill this important gap.

Expenditure patterns of the economically vulnerable elderly are the focus of this chapter. The following sections cover poverty demographics and the distribution of income among the elderly, including discussion of the economic vulnerability of older women; a detailed discussion of two of our empirical studies of expenditures on necessities by vulnerable older households; and our conclusions. In the two empirical studies presented, we first analyze expenditures by older households on the necessity categories of food, housing, and health care,[2] by income level and by household receipt of financial assistance. Second, for the decade of the 1980s, we analyze changes in expenditures on necessities, comparing elderly and nonelderly households.

ECONOMIC VULNERABILITY
OF ELDERLY HOUSEHOLDS

The federally defined poverty level was established in 1963 under the Johnson administration and is still used today for the purpose of establishing eligibility for federal transfer programs. Separate and lower poverty levels were set for elderly than for nonelderly households of the same size. The 1995 poverty level for households with householder age 65 and over was $7,309 for one person and $9,219 for two persons, compared with $7,929 and $10,259 for those under 65 years (U.S. Bureau of the Census, 1996a).

In 1995, incomes of older Americans rose and their poverty rate declined to 10.5 percent, the lowest rate for those aged 65 and over since poverty has been measured. This is less than a third of the 35.2 percent for the elderly in 1959, the first year poverty was measured ("Double-Header," 1996). This is also lower than the nearly 14 percent of the total U.S. population classified as being below the poverty threshold (U.S. Bureau of the Census, 1996a).

The poverty status of the elderly, like that of the nonelderly population, also varies by age and race. For persons considered the young-old (age 65 to 74), the poverty rate is 11 percent; it is 15 percent for those age 75 to 84; and for the old-old (age 85 and over), it is 20 percent (U.S. Bureau of the Census, 1996c). In 1959, 33 percent of white elderly and 63 percent of black elderly were poor. Currently, 9 percent of white elderly, 25 percent of black elderly, and 24 percent of Hispanic elderly are poor (U.S. Bureau of the Census, 1996a).

Between 1980 and 1993, average incomes (in nominal dollars) increased 106 percent for older households, compared to 97 percent for the total population. Although elderly households are now generally at least as well-off as younger households, not all older households are able to maintain economic viability. Further, those who do not fall below the poverty cutoff are more likely to be classified as near poor (with income 100–125 percent of the poverty level) than the nonelderly. This concentration of elderly just over their poverty threshold constitutes almost 20 percent of the near poor (U.S. Department of Commerce, 1996).

It is important to emphasize that the official poverty measure is defined solely in terms of pretax current cash income. While this provides a useful measure of purchasing potential, there are several reasons why this may not give an accurate measure of household well-being, particularly for the elderly. As an annual threshold, the federal definition of poverty gives no indication of whether poverty status in any given year is temporary or more permanent. It also does not provide a measure of consumption or living conditions, and it ignores home ownership and other wealth assets. This has particular relevance for older poor families, 63 percent of whom live in owner-occupied homes (Federman et al., 1996). Further, this measure does not include in-kind transfers, such as food stamps[3] or claims to health care, including Medicare and Medicaid, all of which provide a major transfer benefit to older persons. For these reasons, the federal government calculates alternative definitions of poverty such as definition 14, which encompasses the broadest array of income and in-kind transfers and imputed return on home equity. According to this definition, the poverty rate for the elderly is 5.2 percent, which is considerably lower than the 9.4 percent rate for the overall population.

Entitlements and Safety-Net Programs

Government programs are responsible for a considerable share of the well-being of elderly Americans (Clark and Sumner, 1985). The dramatic reductions in the poverty rates for the elderly were caused in large part by the "catch-up" increases and the indexing of Social Security benefits to inflation rates (U.S. Bureau of the Census, 1996c). While the share of the older population in poverty has declined because of transfer programs, the growth of this demographic group has prevented the number of elderly in poverty from decreasing (Levitan, 1990).

Among U.S. households receiving some form of public assistance, 21 percent are age 65 or older (Passero, 1996). Nearly 40 percent of the elderly are kept out of poverty by receipt of Social Security payments. Social Security constitutes the major source of income (providing over half of all income) for two-thirds of beneficiaries, and it is the only source of income for 14 percent (U.S. Department of Health and Human Services, 1994).

Table 5.1 presents the distribution of entitlement and other safety-net programs for elderly and nonelderly families in 1993. It reveals that over 96 percent of families with a person age 65 and older received at least one government benefit, over 93 percent received two benefits, and over 20 percent received three benefits. This is in contrast to 38 percent, 17 percent, and 10 percent respectively for families without an elderly person. Entitlement benefits and other safety-net programs are generally divided into two categories: work-related benefits, which are based on past work history, and need-related benefits. Almost all families containing an elderly person received at least one work-related government transfer benefit, while a fifth received at least one need-related benefit (Wu, 1995).

Table 5.1 also reveals the dependence of many elderly on safety-net programs for access to the basic necessities of food, housing, and health care. The percent of families with an older person (6 percent) receiving food stamps is only half as large as the percent of other families that receive food stamps (12 percent). However, a larger share of families with an older person benefit from housing assistance. Among households with an older person, 6.4 percent receive public housing and rent subsidies, while only 4.9 percent of nonelderly families receive housing assistance.

The elderly particularly benefit from health care programs. Almost all receive Medicare coverage, and nearly as many receive Medicaid as families without a person age 65 and over. Medicaid eligibility of the elderly was substantially expanded in 1992, when the federal government mandated that Medicare premiums and deductibles would be covered by Medicaid for those who could not afford these payments. In addition, Medicaid coverage is provided for long-term care for impoverished institutionalized elderly.

Table 5.1
Distribution of Entitlement and Other Safety-Net Programs by Age: 1993

	Families with Person Age 65+		Families without Person Age 65+	
	Number (1000s)	Percent (%)	Number (1000s)	Percent (%)
One Benefit	22,516	96.3	33,317	38.2
Two Benefits	21,648	93.2	14,951	17.1
Three Benefits	4,814	20.7	9,353	10.2
Work-related benefits	22,402	96.5	17,431	20.0
Social Security	21,100	90.9	5,458	6.3
Medicare	22,190	95.6	2,608	3.0
Unemployment Compensation	177	0.8	7,670	8.8
Retirement benefits	2,799	12.1	1,486	1.7
Veteran's benefits	918	4.0	967	1.1
Other[a]	766	3.1	2,763	3.2
Need-related benefits	4,642	20.0	23,900	27.4
Medicaid	2,371	10.2	9,607	11.0
Supplemental Security Income	1,337	5.8	2561	2.9
Food stamps	1,373	5.9	10,130	11.6
Energy assistance	1,024	4.4	3,200	3.7
Public housing	1,098	4.7	2,794	3.2
Rent subsidies	398	1.7	1,501	1.7
Veteran's pension	301	1.3	217	0.3
Other[b]	564	2.4	16,362	20.1

[a] Other includes: Worker's Compensation (0.4%), Survivor's benefits (2.4%), Disability insurance (0.4%). Percentages are for families with a person age 65 and above.

[b] Other includes: reduced price or free school lunch (1.9%), AFDC (0.1%), public assistance other than AFDC (0.4%), educational assistance (0.1%). Percentages are for families with a person age 65 and above.

Source: K. B. Wu, 1995, November, Recipiency of entitlement and other safety-net program benefits among families in 1993, *Data Digest*, Public Policy Institute, American Association of Retired Persons. Data derived from the March 1994 Current Population Survey.

A particular problem for impoverished elderly is their inability to change their low-income status. The elderly are considerably less likely to move out of poverty than nonelderly adults, with an exit rate of 14 percent for the elderly compared with 25 percent for nonelderly adults (U.S.

Bureau of the Census, 1996c). This reflects the relative stability of elderly incomes. Once the resources of older persons become exhausted, minimal likelihood exists for them to generate the income necessary to improve their economic status or to leave assistance programs (Hurd, 1990). Opportunities for employment of the elderly diminish, Social Security payments only increase with inflation, many pensions either do not increase or only rise by inflation, and older households are the least likely to inherit. Thus, receipt of public assistance is much more likely to represent a permanent condition for older households, who remain among the most economically vulnerable Americans (Koelln, Rubin, and Picard, 1995).

Income Distribution of the Elderly

Although many older Americans are financially comfortable, with a significant group being well-off, the largest share of the elderly have low incomes. This age-based income inequality persists despite a quarter century of growth of the income transfer programs designed to improve their economic status. While government transfer programs have been the crucial lever in substantially enhancing the well-being of many elderly, some groups among the elderly have not benefitted as much as others. Thus the income distribution of the elderly population remains more unequal than that of the nonelderly (Hurd, 1990; Crystal and Shea, 1990).

Figure 5.1 presents the 1993 income distribution of older households compared with two groups of middle-aged households (ages 45–54 and 55–64) and with the total population. The data reveal the greater concentration of those age 65 and over in lower-income groups relative to households in their preretirement prime earning years and to the total population. Two-thirds of older households have annual income levels below $25,000, whereas only one-fourth of those in the age 45–54 group and one-third in the age 55–64 group have incomes below $25,000 (U. S. Bureau of the Census, 1995).

Economic Vulnerability of Older Women

While older Americans have made substantial income and general economic gains, older single women remain one of the groups most likely to be poor. Women comprise just under 60 percent of the population age 65 and over, but they are nearly three-quarters of the elderly poor. Black women are 5 percent of the elderly, but they are 15 percent of poor elderly. Within each racial or ethnic group, poverty was more prevalent for women than for men both at the beginning and the end of the 1980s (U.S. Bureau of the Census, 1996c).

Figure 5.1
Household Income Distribution by Age Group and Total Population, 1993

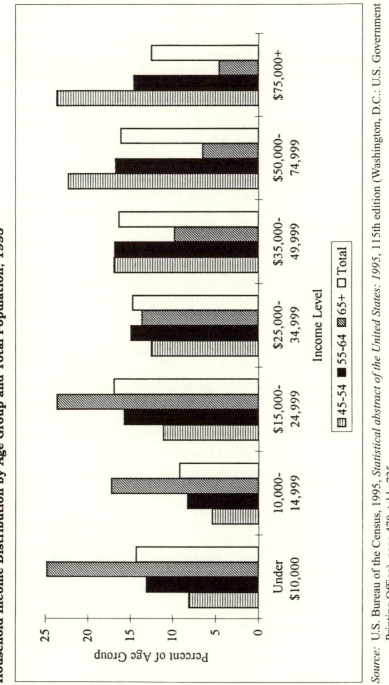

Source: U.S. Bureau of the Census, 1995, *Statistical abstract of the United States: 1995*, 115th edition (Washington, D.C.: U.S. Government Printing Office), page 470, table 725.

Median income and earnings are almost twice as large for older males as for females. Women are much less likely than men to receive private pension benefits, and both average monthly pension income and lump-sum distributions are twice as large for males. Despite the fact that benefits for many women are based on spousal earnings records, Social Security benefits are also considerably higher for males than for females. Nonetheless, Social Security is the major income source of both retired and nonretired single women.

While only 40 percent of women age 65 and over are married, three-fourths of men are married. Almost half of elderly women are widowed (over a third of those age 65 to 74 and two-thirds of those age 75+), compared with less than 15 percent of older men (U.S. Bureau of the Census, 1994c). Marital and family status are major determinants of poverty among older women, and older married women are much more economically secure than those who are single.

The differences in marital status of elderly men and women translate into quite distinct living arrangements. Over two-fifths of older women live alone, and an additional fifth live with someone else. This is considerably more than twice the share of older men either living alone or with someone else (U.S. Bureau of the Census, 1994c). Of 2.3 million elderly living alone, 2 million are women and half of these are termed near poor, having income less than 125 percent of the poverty level (U.S. Bureau of the Census, 1996c).

Measurement of poverty among the elderly is complicated by the 20 percent of elderly women who live with relatives or others. The income of at least a third of these elderly is below the poverty level, but most are not counted as poor (Schulz, 1992). The major reason they live with others is their lack of adequate income to sustain independent housing, but poverty is measured by total household income and does not account for low income of individual household members. Thus, even impoverished elderly persons are unlikely to be counted as poor if they reside in nonpoor households, so official poverty statistics of the elderly understate the case of poor older women (Rubin, 1997).

Rubin and Nieswiadomy (1995) found that older single females are likely to dissave at unsustainable rates to cover their expenditures and that they are relatively worse off than couples or single males. The income of single females was less than half that of married couples, and somewhat over half that of single males. Both retired single males and females spent 12 percent more than their after-tax income.

Overall, the income and financial picture for older single women appears grim, although younger cohorts among elderly women have different patterns than do the more aged. Given their limited past earnings or nonexistent work histories, women's pension income tends to be quite low. They generally own limited financial assets that generate little income. Despite the fact that income is the usual measure of economic viability, wealth may actually provide a better measure for life-cycle considerations, particularly for the elderly, because it measures consumption opportunities (Hurd, 1990).

One of the most notable aspects of expenditure patterns for older women is the large share of spending devoted to housing. This large housing share is generated by utilities and household operations rather than spending on shelter. While single females allocate well over 40 percent of their budgets to housing, single males spend less than 30 percent, comparable to housing expenditures for married couples (Rubin and Nieswiadomy, 1995). Clearly, policies for affordable elderly housing are needed, especially for women. These might include expansion of current programs such as vouchers, subsidies, increased property tax exemptions, or expanded availability of reverse mortgages.

EMPIRICAL ANALYSES—DATA AND METHODOLOGY

We extend previous research with two studies of expenditures on necessities by vulnerable elderly households. We first analyze expenditures on necessities by elderly households in 1990, comparing across income categories and also comparing those receiving and not receiving financial assistance. Second, we analyze necessity expenditures, comparing nonelderly and elderly households and comparing change over the decade of the 1980s between age groups.

Data

The data utilized in both studies are from the Bureau of Labor Statistics (BLS) Consumer Expenditure (CE) Survey interview tapes. The selection criteria for the samples in these two studies are consistent with those outlined in Chapter 1, where the CE Survey is detailed. These criteria include only households that are complete income reporters, with after-tax income greater than zero, and that are living independently. Elderly households have a reference person or spouse age 65 or over. The comparison group of nonelderly households excludes those with an elderly person.

The CE Survey samples were drawn to include only households with a minimum of two quarters of expenditure data, which are annualized by a weighted sum over available quarters. To enhance sample size, the data are pooled for two-year periods, with 1989–1990 being the focus period in both studies, and with 1980–1981 as the comparison period for cross-sectional analysis in the second study. However, we refer to these pooled years of data as 1980 or 1990 data to simplify our discussion and the tables.

Income and expenditure data for 1980 and 1981 are inflation adjusted to 1990 levels, using the Consumer Price Index (CPI) to make all data compatible in constant 1990 dollars.[4] This enables comparisons over time in terms of the general price level, and it allows discussion of the findings in real, or inflation-adjusted, values.

The necessity expenditure categories analyzed are food, housing, and health care. In addition, we analyze either total expenditures or other expenditures. The BLS classifications were used to define the three categories of necessities. Food expenditure includes food at home and food away from home. In the CE data base, expenditures on food indicate the value of food purchased, including that paid for with subsidized food stamps, rather than just the amount spent above the value of food stamps. Housing consists of rent or mortgage payments, utilities, household operations, and house furnishings and equipment.[5] Health care includes out-of-pocket expenditures on health insurance, prescription drugs, medical supplies, medical services (hospital, physician, and other services), and other health care.[6]

In both studies described, income distribution is determined using the 1990 federal poverty level for elderly and nonelderly households, adjusted for family size. For households of the same size, the poverty level is lower for the elderly than the nonelderly. The 1990 poverty level for age 65 and over is $5,767 for one-person households and $7,237 for two-person households, compared to $6,257 for one-person and $7,829 for two-person nonelderly households (U.S. Bureau of the Census, 1993). Consistent with earlier studies by Wilensky (1982) and Smeeding (1989), the three income categories defined for both analyses are poor (less than 125 percent of the poverty level), low income (between 125 percent and 200 percent of the poverty level), and higher income (more than 200 percent of the poverty level).

Methodology

In both studies, descriptive statistics are used first to compare the mean values and budget shares of out-of-pocket expenditures on necessities among the groups of older households. Second, two-stage least squares regression models are developed to analyze patterns of elderly household expenditures on necessities.

Two-stage regression is used to analyze the relationships between the dependent variables (expenditures on three categories of necessities) and the explanatory socioeconomic variables, because both expenditures and any income measure are endogenous variables and would be simultaneously determined. Ordinary least squares estimates would produce biased coefficients, as total expenditures are simultaneously determined with expenditures on certain categories (Liviatan, 1961).

The underlying theory of consumer decision making, outlined in Chapter 1, provides the theoretical rationale for this approach. The Life Cycle Hypothesis (Ando and Modigliani, 1963) and the Permanent Income Hypothesis (Friedman, 1957) posit that rational consumers maximize utility by leveling consumption over time. Thus, consumers ignore the fluctuations of current income around what is termed permanent income in order to smooth variations in consumption.

In the first stage of the two-stage least squares regressions, the permanent income variable is estimated for application in the second stage of the model. Since permanent income is not observable, we use total expenditures as the most acceptable proxy for permanent income. Total expenditures are highly correlated with permanent income without reflecting the year-to-year fluctuations in current income.[7]

To estimate permanent income, we regress total expenditures on current income, financial assets, and education and the other demographic and economic variables that are included in the second stage. The second-stage variables used to explain the three expenditure categories of necessities are: a constant, the log of predicted permanent income, age of reference person, and family size, and dummy variables for race, housing tenure, and receipt of cash financial assistance (AFDC and/or SSI) and food stamps.

In the second study, which compares change over time, two additional dummy variables are used to analyze the change in expenditures on necessities over the 1980s. The COMPARE variable indicates the time period in which the sample household was selected, taking a value of 1 for households in 1990 and 0 for those in 1980. The FA*COMPARE variable indicates household receipt of financial assistance, with a value of 1 if the household receives aid in 1990 and 0 otherwise. Therefore, the coefficient on COMPARE presents a measure of change in spending by household i on necessity category j over the 1980s. Similarly, the coefficient on FA*COMPARE indicates whether recipient household i had different spending patterns on necessity category j in 1990 than in 1980.

In both studies, household economic status is indicated by receipt of transfer benefits, denoted by the food stamps and cash assistance variables.

There are two reasons we do not use health care assistance parameters as an indicator of economic status. First, as noted above, Medicare is virtually universal for those over 65. Second, since eligibility for Medicaid is determined by receipt of AFDC, these two programs are codetermined and could cause problems of multicollinearity. The base case is a nonwhite household, occupying rental housing, and not receiving financial assistance or food stamps.

The general linear form of the second stage model for household i and expenditure category j is:

$$EN_{ij} = \sum_{K=1}^{8} \beta_{kj} X_{ik} + \epsilon_{ij}.$$

The dependent variables, EN_{ij}, are the natural log (ln) of annual expenditures on the three necessity expenditure categories (food, housing, and health care). These variables are regressed on a matrix (X_{ik}) of k explanatory variables. For the dummy variables: race equals 0 for non-white, 1 for white; housing tenure equals 0 for renters, 1 for owners; financial assistance equals 0 for nonrecipients, 1 for recipients; food stamps equals 0 for nonrecipients of food stamps, 1 for recipients. The structural parameters (β_{kj}) indicate the relationship between the dependent and explanatory variables for the different income categories. The error term, ϵ_{ij}, is assumed to be normally distributed.

In the first empirical study presented, the regression model is estimated for the three expenditure categories, for each of the three income categories, and for the total sample. The model is not estimated for the financial assistance category, because we test the significance of this parameter, which indicates the sensitivity of expenditures on necessities to receipt of public assistance. Thus, financial assistance serves as a dummy variable in the specification of the regression model for the three different income categories and for the total sample. In the second study, the model is estimated for elderly and nonelderly households, with the two additional parameters (the COMPARE and FA*COMPARE variables) described above for comparison of two time periods.

The log form of both expenditures and permanent income is used to improve the fit. And this double-log form gives an important property to the model: the coefficient on permanent income represents an income elasticity, such that a β_{kj} percentage increase in expenditure on food, housing, or health care is generated by a 1 percent increase in permanent income. For example, it might be used to test the impact of a policy change, such as how a housing subsidy affects spending on other goods.

EXPENDITURES ON NECESSITIES:
EMPIRICAL STUDY I

Because earlier empirical studies of expenditures on basic necessities have been limited, this research information is needed for consideration of the quality of life of elderly households and for policy development affecting this rapidly growing segment of the population. In this section, we compare expenditures on necessities by older Americans receiving cash assistance (AFDC and/or SSI) with expenditures of elderly nonrecipients. This enables us to compare those with income assistance to poor nonrecipients and also to those who are not economically disadvantaged. This research provides detailed information on necessity expenditures with emphasis on the most vulnerable, poor and low-income older households. This section is based on a study published in the *Social Science Quarterly*.[8]

Sample Characteristics

The economic and demographic characteristics of the selected CE Survey sample of elderly households provide the foundation for this study. Sample groups are determined first by receipt or nonreceipt of cash assistance. Second, nonrecipients are disaggregated into three income categories based on the federal poverty level for older households and adjusted for family size. The three income categories defined are: poor (less than 125 percent of the poverty level), low income (between 125 percent and 200 percent of the poverty level), and higher income (more than 200 percent of the poverty level).

Several key differences are found when elderly households receiving financial assistance are compared with poor nonrecipients. Those in the poor category are somewhat better educated and are more likely to be white and home owners than those receiving financial assistance. Both low-income and higher-income elderly households are even more likely to be white, home owners, and have higher levels of education than poor. Home ownership increases about 10 percent per group, moving from assistance recipients (54 percent) to poor (64 percent), low income (74 percent) and higher income (86 percent).[9]

Average age of the reference person for recipients in the poor group is 75, compared with 74 for low-income households and 72 for higher-income households. This gives an indication that some households become more poor as they age. Even more substantial differences exist in the marital status of the different groups. Among assistance recipients, 21 percent are married. Among nonrecipients, the percent of households that are married varies from one-fourth for poor households to 44 percent for low-income to 63 percent for higher-income elderly.

The reported average income level reflects cash income (including cash transfers) and the value of food stamps. Food stamps are received by 39 percent of those on cash assistance, by 11 percent of poor nonrecipients, and by 2 percent of the low-income group. Among income assistance recipients, 83 percent receive SSI and 21 percent receive AFDC, with a limited number of households getting both.

Findings

Table 5.2 presents average incomes, expenditures, and budget shares on the necessity categories of food, housing, and health care for elderly households receiving financial assistance and for the three income groups of nonrecipients. Mean household pretax income of assistance recipients is $9,685, which is more than 50 percent higher than the average income of poor nonrecipients ($6,121).[10] Further, the mean level of assets of recipients ($4,589) is surprisingly close to that of the poor households ($4,619). Average pretax income of the low-income group is $11,201 and for the higher-income group is $30,303.

Both older assistance recipients and the poor group spend 40 percent of their total expenditures on housing; however, those on assistance spend 28 percent on food, while the poor group spends 22 percent on food. The poor group spends 14 percent on health care, compared to less than 9 percent for aid recipients, which reflects the Medicaid eligibility of both AFDC and SSI recipients and the comprehensiveness of Medicaid coverage. The low-income group has the highest health care expenditure share (15 percent). Overall, expenditures on necessities increase as income level increases; but at higher levels of income, the budget shares on necessities are lower.

When income and expenditures are compared, the data suggest that poor and low-income nonrecipients may not be as well-off as cash assistance recipients. The reported after-tax income of cash aid recipients ($9,578) is slightly greater than their total expenditures ($9,241). In contrast, the poor and low-income groups appear to be dissaving at unsustainable rates.[11] Poor nonrecipients spend almost twice ($12,042) their after-tax income ($6,102), and those in the low-income group spend ($14,711), almost one-third more than their after-tax income ($11,039).

These findings for the poor and low-income groups are consistent with the prediction of the Life Cycle Hypothesis described in Chapter 1. This theory of consumption and saving indicates that households will dissave in their later years in order to smooth their level of consumption over time.

Table 5.2
Average Income, Necessity Expenditures, and Budget Shares
of Elderly Households by Income Level: 1990

	Financial Assistance Recipients[b]	Nonassistance recipients: Income as a % of Poverty Level			Total Sample
		Poor < 125%	Low Income 125-200%	Higher Income > 200%	
Average Income					
Before taxes	$9,685	$6,121	$11,201	$30,303	$19,662
After taxes	9,578	6,102	11,039	28,271	18,598
Financial Assets	$4,589	$4,619	$11,614	$34,803	$21,353
Food Stamps	39%	11%	2%	0%	6%
Currently working	9%	14%	11%	29%	20%
Average Expenditures					
Food	$2,300	$2,299	$2,845	$4,068	$3,312
Housing	3,609	4,517	4,793	7,025	5,769
Health Care	762	1,517	2,082	2,499	2,087
Total Expenditure	9,241	12,042	14,711	24,502	18,697
Budget Shares					
Food	0.28	0.22	0.21	0.18	0.20
Housing	0.40	0.40	0.35	0.31	0.34
Health Care	0.09	0.14	0.15	0.12	0.13
Sample Size	96	253	317	664	1330

[a] The poverty level is based on household size for each consumer unit. The elderly poverty level in 1990 was $5,767 for one person and was $7,237 for households with two persons.

[b] Financial Assistance includes recipients of Aid to Families with Dependent Children (AFDC) or Supplemental Security Income (SSI).

Source: K. Koelln, R. M. Rubin, and M. S. Picard, 1995, Vulnerable elderly households: Expenditures on necessities by older Americans, *Social Science Quarterly*, 76(3): 619–633. Reprinted by permission of the University of Texas Press.

The data suggest that government assistance allows elderly recipients to avoid dissaving, as their average asset level is almost the same as those in the poor group. In contrast, higher-income elderly continue to accumulate positive savings, as their income ($28,271) exceeds their expenditures ($24,502). For the higher-income group, these findings may indicate a bequest motive or uncertainty about their life span, and are consistent with alternative consumption theories such as Deaton's (1992) or Frank's (1985) positional goods theory, mentioned in Chapter 1. Thus, our findings indicate that a single theory of consumption and saving is unlikely to satisfactorily explain the behavior of all older households. This is consistent with findings of the heterogeneity of elderly households and particularly reflects the diversity of their financial situations in later life.

Regression Results

Table 5.3 presents second-stage regression results for the three categories of necessity expenditures by income level and for the total sample.[12] Permanent income is highly significant and positive for food expenditures by all income groups except the poor, and its coefficient is significantly less than one for all income categories. For example, the permanent income coefficient for the low-income group indicates that a 1 percent increase in income generates a .5 percent increase in spending on food. As income increases, the budget share on food decreases. Food stamps reduce out-of-pocket expenditures on food for the poor households by 15 percent. For all income groups, food expenditure decreases 1 percent for each year of age of the reference person. Family size has a positive and highly significant effect on food expenditures, with the most pronounced effect on poor households, where spending on food increases 28 percent for each one-person increase in family size.

Housing expenditures are significantly impacted by permanent income and housing tenure for all elderly income categories. In contrast to our finding for food, we find that as income increases for the poor and low-income groups, spending on housing increases proportionately to the increase in income. This is indicated by the permanent income parameters for housing equalling approximately one. In contrast, for the higher-income category and the total sample, the income coefficient for housing is significantly less than one. The data indicate that renters spend more on housing than owners. Unlike the poor group, family size is significant and negative for housing expenditures for the low- and higher-income elderly households.

Since health care spending is more variable and random than spending on other necessities, it is more difficult to predict than expenditures on food and housing, as shown by the adjusted R^2s. Prediction of health care expenditures is further complicated by the lack of health status variables in the CE Survey data base. As a determinant of out-of-pocket expenditures on health care, the permanent income parameter is significant for the poor and higher-income elderly, as well as for the total sample. Financial assis-

Table 5.3
Regression Results for Necessities for Elderly by Income Level: 1990

Necessity Category	Income as a Percent of Poverty Level			Total Sample
	<125%	125%-200	>200%	
Ln(Food):				
Constant	7.87 *	2.96 *	2.44 *	2.34 *
ln(Permanent Income)	0.00	0.55 *	0.61 *	0.61 *
Age (reference)	-0.01 *	-0.01 *	-0.01 *	-0.01 *
Family Size	0.28 *	0.12 *	0.11 *	0.11 *
Race (reference)	0.14 *	0.13 *	0.10	0.07 *
Housing Tenure	0.02	0.11 *	0.07 *	0.05 *
Financial Assistance	0.03	-0.08	0.09	0.13 *
Food Stamps	-0.15 *	0.03	-0.02	0.02
Adjusted R^2	0.33	0.39	0.44	0.54
F value	23.18 *	30.97 *	76.10 *	219.78 *
Ln(Housing):				
Constant	-0.95 *	-2.19	0.52	0.44
ln(Permanent Income)	0.95 *	1.15 *	0.84 *	0.85 *
Age (reference)	0.01 *	0.00	0.00	0.00 *
Family Size	-0.05	-0.19 *	-0.06 *	-0.07 *
Race (reference)	-0.12 *	-0.15 *	0.08	-0.05
Housing Tenure	-0.23 *	-0.24 *	-0.28	-0.24 *
Financial Assistance	-0.04	0.16	0.23 *	0.02
Food Stamps	-0.04	0.33 *	0.08	0.00
Adjusted R^2	0.38	0.20	0.36	0.46
F value	28.81 *	12.73 *	54.60 *	160.01 *
Ln(Health Care):				
Constant	-5.69	2.44	1.77	-1.01
ln(Permanent Income)	1.12 *	0.41	0.37 *	0.66 *
Age (reference)	0.03 *	0.01	0.02 *	0.02 *
Family Size	-0.27 *	0.13	0.13 *	0.03
Race (reference)	0.23	0.25	0.15	0.21 *
Housing Tenure	0.39 *	0.20	0.22 *	0.26 *
Financial Assistance	-0.44 *	-0.88 *	-0.48 *	-0.61 *
Food Stamps	0.27	-0.08	-0.07	0.01
Adjusted R^2	0.16	0.06	0.09	0.19
F value	9.89 *	4.11 *	10.96 *	44.45 *

*Statistically significant at $p<0.10$. All F values are significant at $p<0.01$.

Source: K. Koelln, R. M. Rubin, and M. S. Picard, 1995, Vulnerable elderly households: Expenditures on necessities by older Americans, *Social Science Quarterly*, 76(3): 619–633. Reprinted by permission of the University of Texas Press.

tance is significant and negative for all income categories, and it is the sole significant predictor for the low-income households. Receipt of financial assistance, for the total sample, permits 61 percent less spending on health care than for the elderly without financial aid. Also, health care spending increases about 2 percent for each additional year of age.

Overall, as income increases, the budget share on food decreases for all three income categories, differing from budget shares for housing and health care. A 1 percent increase in income generates approximately a corresponding 1 percent increase in spending on housing for all three income groups. For health care, a 1 percent increase in income generates about a 1 percent increase in spending for the poor, no significant change for the low-income group, and a .37 percent increase for those with higher income.

ELDERLY AND NONELDERLY EXPENDITURES ON NECESSITIES OVER THE 1980s: EMPIRICAL STUDY II

The study presented in this section expands the analysis just presented with comparisons over the decade of the 1980s and comparisons of elderly and nonelderly households, grouped on the basis of receipt or nonreceipt of financial assistance. Mean expenditures and budget shares on categories of necessities are compared across time by age group. This comparison answers the broad research question: What changes occurred in expenditures on necessities by elderly households compared with the nonelderly during the 1980s? This section is based on a study published in the *Monthly Labor Review*.[13]

Sample Characteristics

For each of the two time periods (1980 and 1990), we define four sample groups based on age and receipt of financial assistance. We compare elderly households (with a reference person or spouse age 65 or over) with nonelderly households. Households with a resident elderly person who is not the reference person or spouse are excluded from the sample. The effects of cash transfer payments on household spending patterns are emphasized to analyze the socioeconomic factors that affect expenditures on necessities. As above, receipt of SSI or AFDC defines recipients of financial assistance.

Overall, for both time periods, households receiving financial assistance have substantially less income and less financial assets, are more frequently non-white, have lower levels of education, and are less likely to be home owners, compared with nonrecipients. In both 1980 and 1990, elderly assistance recipients are more likely to be single, and nonelderly are mostly single-parent households. Nonrecipients are twice as likely as recipients to be a married couple. These demographic factors relating to family type are somewhat mandated by the assistance eligibility criteria, which determine the group composition.

Among those under age 65, assistance recipients are twice as likely as nonrecipients not to have completed high school, but 40 percent of recipients in 1980 and 52 percent in 1990 are high school graduates. Lack of a high school education is much greater among elderly aid recipients (89 percent in 1980 and 71 percent in 1990), compared with 59 percent and 45 percent of the nonrecipients. Thus, lack of educational attainment appears to be a major factor across the decade in the determination of low income.

For both time periods, households receiving financial assistance have less than half the before- or after-tax income of nonrecipients, as shown in Table 5.4. Among the nonelderly, recipients have one-fourth the level of financial assets of nonrecipients, but among the elderly, recipients have only 7 percent of the assets of nonrecipients in 1980 and 20 percent in 1990.

Since home ownership constitutes the major asset of most American households, it is an important characteristic when comparing the economic viability of household groups. For nonrecipients in both 1980 and 1990, two-thirds of nonelderly and about three-fourths of elderly are home owners. In contrast, for those receiving financial assistance only slightly over one-fourth of nonelderly and approximately half of elderly households own homes.

From 1980 to 1990, the share of elderly with incomes below 125 percent of the poverty level declined for both those households that received financial assistance (from 82 to 71 percent) and those not receiving assistance (from 36 to 20 percent). For nonelderly nonrecipients, the decline was from 15 to 12 percent. Over the decade, the share of nonrecipients with higher incomes (over 200 percent of the poverty level) increased from 69 to 75 percent for nonelderly and from 39 to 54 percent for elderly. But the share of recipients with higher incomes remained 17 percent for nonelderly recipients, while it increased from 3 percent to 14 percent for the elderly.

Among nonelderly recipients, the share receiving food stamps declined slightly over the decade from 73 to 69 percent, while it decreased from 50 percent to 39 percent for elderly recipient households. Only 3 to 4 percent of nonrecipients in both age groups received food stamps in either time period.

Table 5.4
Necessity Expenditures of Nonelderly and Elderly Households by Financial Assistance Status: 1980 and 1990 (1990 Dollars)

CATEGORY	NONELDERLY			ELDERLY		
	1980	1990	%Change	1980	1990	%Change
NONRECIPIENTS OF FINANCIAL ASSISTANCE						
Mean Income						
Before Taxes	$30,427	$37,623	23.7	$15,537	$20,438	31.5
After Taxes	26,520	33,519	26.4	14,557	19,299	32.6
Total Expenditure	25,883	31,468	21.6	15,071	19,432	28.9
Mean Assets	5,679	10,231	80.2	10,781	22,657	110.2
Avg. Expenditure						
Food	4,870	4,800	-1.4	3,160	3,391	7.3
Housing	7,158	9,528	33.1	4,849	5,937	22.4
Health	968	1,236	27.7	1,548	2,190	41.5
Other	12,887	15,904	23.4	5,514	7,914	43.5
Budget Share						
Food	18.8	15.3	-18.6	21.0	17.5	-16.7
Housing	27.7	30.3	9.4	32.2	30.6	-5.0
Health	3.7	3.9	5.4	10.3	11.3	9.7
Other	49.8	50.5	1.4	36.6	40.7	11.2
Sample Size (N)	3,837	4,279		989	1,234	
RECIPIENTS OF FINANCIAL ASSISTANCE						
Mean Income						
Before Taxes	14,137	15,147	7.1	6,856	9,685	41.3
After Taxes	13,451	14,613	8.6	6,832	9,578	40.2
Total Expenditure	13,579	15,879	16.9	7,542	9,242	22.5
Mean Assets	1,410	2,652	88.1	730	4,589	528.6
Avg. Expenditure						
Food	3,675	3,723	1.3	2,355	2,300	-2.3
Housing	4,394	5,375	22.3	2,640	3,609	36.7
Health	319	474	48.6	544	762	40.1
Other	5,191	6,299	21.3	2,003	2,571	28.4
Budget Share						
Food	27.1	23.5	-13.3	31.2	24.9	-20.2
Housing	32.4	33.9	4.6	35.0	39.0	11.4
Health	2.3	3.0	30.4	7.2	8.2	13.9
Other	38.2	39.7	3.9	26.6	27.8	4.5
Sample Size (N)	306	315		125	96	

Source: R. M. Rubin and K. Koelln, 1996, Elderly and nonelderly expenditures on necessities in the 1980s, *Monthly Labor Review*, 119(9): 24–31.

Findings

Table 5.4 presents mean household expenditures and budget shares by age group, financial assistance status, and time period for the three necessity categories of food, housing, and health care and other (discretionary) spending. The percent changes in expenditures and budget shares during the 1980s are also shown. We expect mean expenditures on each category to increase over time, as real income (in constant 1990 dollars) grew substantially for all household groups except nonelderly financial assistance recipients.[14] However, we found, as expected, the largest share of increased real income was allocated to other (or discretionary) spending, because as incomes increase, expenditures on basic necessities meet household needs. Food prices did not increase as rapidly as the overall CPI during the decade of the 1980s (35.5 percent versus 43.8 percent), which probably explains the decrease in constant dollar expenditure on food (U.S. Bureau of the Census, 1993). This is seen in the decline over the 1980s in food expenditure as a share of total expenditures.

In contrast to the relatively low price increases for food over the 1980s, health care prices suffered high inflation (96.4 percent compared to 43.8 percent for the overall CPI) (U.S. Bureau of the Census, 1993). The high health care inflation combined with increased purchases of health care is shown in the increased constant dollar expenditures on health care over the decade for each of the groups. For both groups of elderly (recipients and nonrecipients) in 1980 and 1990, the budget share on health care is substantially higher than that for the nonelderly. In addition, in all cases, the elderly spend a slightly larger share on housing than the nonelderly. The group with the lowest income, elderly assistance recipients, had the largest budget share on housing (35 percent in 1980 and 39 percent in 1990).

We use the amount and share of total spending on non-necessities (other goods and services), as a measure of household welfare (i.e., well-being).[15] By this measure, all household groups are generally better off by the end of the decade, consistent with the increases in real income seen in Table 5.4. Elderly households gained relative to the nonelderly over the decade, and this gain is largely attributable to their decreased food shares. The data further indicate that the welfare gains of households without financial assistance were larger than the gains of recipients. In particular, elderly nonrecipients experienced significant increases in welfare as they were able to spend 44 percent more (real dollars) on other goods and services in 1990 compared to 1980.

Another measure of well-being is the household savings, measured by the difference between after-tax income and total expenditures (Table 5.4).

This measure also gives an indication of the extent to which the household can aspire to maintain its lifestyle. We find that elderly nonrecipients dissaved (i.e., spent more than their income) in both 1980 and 1990. In 1980, elderly aid recipients were dissavers, but by 1990 this situation had changed. In contrast, for the nonelderly, in both periods nonrecipients were net savers and recipients were dissavers.

Regression Results

The second-stage regression results for the three categories of expenditures on necessities by elderly and nonelderly households are shown in Table 5.5. While the significant COMPARE parameters indicate change occurred over the decade of the 1980s for all three necessity expenditure categories and for both age groups, the sign varies among the different categories of spending. The parameter for change is positive for housing for both age groups (indicating around a 6 to 10 percent increase), but it is negative for food (roughly an 8 percent decline) for both age groups and for nonelderly health care (a 9 percent decline). Notably, cash assistance had a significant and positive effect on food but a negative effect on health care spending, for older households in both 1980 and 1990, as shown by the significant financial assistance parameter and nonsignificant FA*COMPARE parameter. The largest change occurred for health care expenditures for the elderly. The coefficient on COMPARE (0.34) indicates that the demand for health care expenditures increased 34 percent over the decade, ceteris paribus. This is an incredibly large increase in demand over a 10-year period.

For food purchases, for both elderly and nonelderly households, the estimate of income elasticity, given by the permanent income parameter, is highly significant and positive but less than one. The nonsignificant FA*COMPARE parameter for the elderly indicates that there was no change over the decade in the relationship between the receipt of financial assistance and spending on food. The financial assistance parameters for the nonelderly indicate that receipt of cash assistance was not an important determinant of spending on food in 1980, but by 1990 financial assistance recipients were spending 7.6 percent more on food than nonrecipients. The food stamp parameter is not significant for elderly households for any of the categories of necessities or for the nonelderly for expenditures on food. This parameter estimate may be a result of the CE data base definition of expenditures on food, which includes food purchased with food stamps rather than the amount spent exclusive of the value of food stamps.

For housing for both age groups, the permanent income parameter values are closer to one than they are for food, indicating that housing is less

Table 5.5
**Regression Results for Necessity Expenditures of Nonelderly and El-
derly Households: 1980 and 1990**

Dependent Variables:	ln(Food)	ln(Housing)	ln(Health Care)
Nonelderly Households:			
Constant	2.224 *	-1.986 *	-11.468 *
Ln(Permanent Income)	0.552 *	1.095 *	1.544 *
Age (reference)	0.006 *	-0.004 *	0.031 *
Family Size	0.112 *	-0.034 *	0.058 *
Race (reference)	0.026 *	-0.082 *	0.451 *
Housing Tenure	0.001	-0.035 *	0.231 *
Food Stamps	-0.004	0.146 *	-0.389 *
Financial Assistance	0.008	0.200 *	-0.662 *
FA*COMPARE	0.076 *	-0.079 *	-0.201
COMPARE	-0.082 *	0.100 *	-0.091 *
Adjusted R^2	0.535	0.499	0.262
F value	1117.421 *	967.651 *	344.778 *
Elderly Households:			
Constant	2.468 *	0.243	-1.765 *
ln(Permanent Income)	0.595 *	0.847 *	0.681 *
Age (reference)	-0.007 *	0.004 *	0.021 *
Family Size	0.125 *	-0.073 *	0.049 *
Race (reference)	0.071 *	0.004	0.309 *
Housing Tenure	0.033 *	-0.191 *	0.328 *
Food Stamps	0.013	0.010	-0.044
Financial Assistance	0.083 *	-0.030	-0.714 *
FA*COMPARE	0.013	0.039	0.151
COMPARE	-0.080 *	0.060 *	0.340 *
Adjusted R^2	0.515	0.450	0.253
F value	289.008 *	223.314 *	92.886 *

* Statistically significant at $p<0.10$. The sample sizes are n = 8116 for nonelderly and n = 2223 for elderly households.

Source: R. M. Rubin and K. Koelln, 1996, Elderly and nonelderly expenditures on necessities in the 1980s, *Monthly Labor Review*, 119(9): 24–31.

of a necessity than food. The positive and significant financial assistance parameter for the nonelderly indicates that receiving cash assistance leads to a 20 percent increase in spending on housing. The significant decrease (8 percent) during the decade indicates that this effect weakened, but the sum of the two parameters remained positive and substantially above zero. For elderly households, financial assistance had no significant effect on housing expenditures, possibly reflecting a level of home ownership twice as high in 1990 for elderly financial aid recipients (54 percent) as for nonelderly recipients (27 percent). However, for the nonelderly, receipt of food stamps leads to a significant increase in housing spending, which may reflect a transfer of funds freed from food spending to housing.

Regression results provide a greater contrast by age group for medical care expenditures than for food or housing. For the nonelderly, the permanent income parameter is substantially greater than one, indicating their purchases of health care are perceived as non-necessities. However, this value is considerably less than one for the elderly, indicating that their health care expenditures are necessities. For both age groups, the financial assistance parameters for health care are significant and negative, and also do not change significantly over the 1980s, indicating that elderly and nonelderly households with financial assistance spend less on health care. This probably reflects mandated Medicaid coverage for those on AFDC and most aged, blind, or disabled recipients of SSI (Schulz, 1992).[16] Our finding that receipt of food stamps is related to a reduction in health care spending for nonelderly households may also reflect program eligibility criteria.

CONCLUSIONS AND POLICY IMPLICATIONS

Despite the rapid growth of cohorts of older Americans, their expenditures on basic needs (food, housing, and health care) have been insufficiently studied as a measure of their economic vulnerability. The two empirical studies in this chapter demonstrate the financial heterogeneity of elderly households and the need to analyze their expenditure patterns by receipt of cash assistance as well as by income level. We considered three income groups, poor (<125 percent of poverty level), lower income (125–200 percent), and higher income (>200 percent). Elderly households with incomes less than 200 percent of the poverty level spend almost three-fourths of their budgets on necessities, whether they receive aid or not. Viewing expenditures on necessities as an indicator of quality of life, a significant share of poor and low-income elderly will require cash or in-kind government assistance in the future.

Our analyses indicate that poor and low-income older households that do not receive cash assistance are even more financially distressed than those receiving transfers. Their reported current income is substantially lower than their expenditures, so they dissave at unsustainable rates. This annual dissaving, combined with their relatively low levels of financial assets, indicates continuing financial exigency.

Our conclusions regarding dissaving by elderly households relate particularly to the three economic theories of household expenditure patterns over time, outlined in Chapter 1. Our findings for the poor and low-income household groups reinforce the Life Cycle or Permanent Income Hypothesis. However, for higher-income elderly, the results validate the precautionary motive for saving emphasized in an alternative theory. Frank's (1985) positional goods theory seems to best explain why the poor spend proportionately larger amounts than higher-income households. Thus, we emphasize the importance of disaggregating by income level to analyze expenditure patterns of elderly households.

Food is a necessity for both the nonelderly and elderly. However, food spending declines 1 percent for each year of age of the elderly but increases 1 percent for each year of age of the nonelderly. We find that food spending is higher for both elderly and nonelderly whites and that it fell for both groups from 1980 to 1990. For the poor elderly, the budget share increases for health care as income rises, and for the low-income elderly, the share spent on housing increases as income rises. For the other income groups, the shares spent on housing and health care decrease as income rises. Housing is a luxury good (income elasticity >1) for the nonelderly and for the low-income elderly and is close to luxury classification for the poor and high-income elderly. For nonelderly households, receipt of financial assistance allows higher housing expenditures in both 1980 and 1990, but no similar effect is found for the elderly. Housing expenditures increase with age for the nonelderly but decrease for the elderly.

In both time periods, receipt of financial assistance reduces out-of-pocket expenditures on health care for both elderly and nonelderly households. This is probably caused by Medicaid eligibility being generally coincident with receipt of SSI or AFDC. Health care is a luxury good for the nonelderly and the poor elderly. But the income elasticity is low for the low-income and higher-income elderly. From 1980 to 1990, health care spending increased 34 percent for the elderly but declined 9 percent for the nonelderly.

Overall, we conclude that well-being increased over the 1980s for the population, as measured by both real income and discretionary spending. The well-being of older households increased relatively more than that of the nonelderly, but assistance recipients experienced relatively smaller increases than nonrecipients. Although both elderly and nonelderly assistance recipients slightly reduced the shares of their budgets spent on necessities over the 1980s, their well-being did not improve as much as that of other households. Real income grew only slightly for nonelderly recipients of cash assistance, while other groups fared much better. The primary reasons for these improvements in household well-being are the increased real incomes and decreased relative price of food.

The plight of economically vulnerable older Americans is highlighted in these findings, which detail their difficulty financing the three basic categories of necessities. We find clear differentials in expenditures on necessities between the poor elderly who are financial assistance recipients and nonrecipients. These results have important implications for a wide range of social welfare issues, such as income distribution, food stamps, housing, and health care policies.

NOTES

1. In 1959, 33.1 percent of white elderly and 62.5 percent of black elderly were poor. By 1992, 10.9 percent of white elderly, 33.3 percent of black elderly, and 22.0 percent of Hispanic elderly were poor (U.S. Bureau of the Census, 1996c).

2. We utilize the BLS categories of food, housing, and health care as necessities, although we recognize that some expenditures in these categories may not be necessities for some households and that some expenditures in our residual or "other" category could be considered necessities.

3. Criteria for eligibility for food stamps include household income below the poverty level. Over 1.2 million persons age 65 and over receive food stamps, and most of these recipients are older women living alone (U.S. Bureau of the Census, 1996d).

4. The overall CPI was 90.9 for 1981 and 130.7 for 1990 (U.S. Bureau of the Census, 1996d).

5. The category of housing expenditures does not include payments for nursing home residents, who are not included in the CE Survey.

6. Health care expenditures include household out-of-pocket payments for health goods and services and insurance premiums, but do not include third-party payments.

7. Prais and Houthakker (1955) found that using total expenditures rather than income produces a better fit when predicting some specific expenditure categories. Further, income data on the CE tapes are collected for the prior year and only in the fifth interview, while expenditure data are collected at each interview for the prior quarter. For these reasons, total expenditures provides the preferred surrogate for permanent income. For earlier examples of this procedure, see: McConnel and Deljavan, 1983; Jacobs, Shipp, and Brown, 1989; Rubin and Koelln, 1993; Nieswiadomy and Rubin, 1995; Rubin and Nieswiadomy, 1994.

8. Kenneth Koelln, Rose M. Rubin, and Marion Smith Picard, 1995, Vulnerable elderly households: Expenditures on necessities by older Americans, *Social Science Quarterly,* 76(3): 619–633.

9. We found a 76 percent home ownership rate for the entire sample, which is virtually identical to the 75 percent rate reported for the United States for house-holders age 65 and over ("Elderly Homeownership Rate Increases," 1995).

10. Mean household pretax income of assistance recipients exclusive of cash assistance is $7,649, which is also higher than the average income of poor non-recipients.

11. This dissaving is based on reported current income, recognizing that income might not be fully reported (as in any data base) and that the comparison between income and expenditures does not encompass either financial assets or the value of housing.

12. Because receipt of financial assistance is used as an independent variable, there is no group of assistance recipients in the regression analysis.

13. Rose M. Rubin and Kenneth Koelln, 1996, Elderly and nonelderly expenditures on necessities in the 1980s. *Monthly Labor Review*, 119(9): 24–31.

14. Declining real income is expected for nonelderly assistance recipients, because AFDC payments increase only by action of state legislatures, which rarely occurred during the 1980s. In contrast, for elderly assistance recipients, SSI increases with the CPI, so real income is expected to be constant.

15. The share of total expenditures spent on necessities (or conversely, the share available for other non-necessity expenditures) is used as an economic indicator of household quality of life. Higher shares spent on necessities imply a lower quality of life. This is consistent with the approach suggested by Acs and Sabelhaus (1995, page 44), who indicate that a measure of total expenditure "can be thought of as a 'cash-basis' consumption value, which is not an optimal indicator of economic well-being, but the best measure available at the household level."

16. It was not until 1992 that Congress mandated Medicaid coverage of most out-of-pocket expenses for impoverished Medicare beneficiaries.

Chapter 6

Health Expenditures

National health care expenditures were $989 billion in 1995, or some 13 percent of GDP, with 19 percent of this total paid out-of-pocket by America's households (Levit et al., 1996). Even as health care expenditures have accelerated over time, the percentage of the total paid out-of-pocket by households declined for over two decades, following the 1965 introduction of Medicare and Medicaid and the expansion of employer-sponsored insurance. Currently, however, as government and business strive to control rising health care costs, this trend is being reversed. As delivery sites are shifted from inpatient to outpatient, as third-party coverage shifts increasingly to managed care, and as cost sharing increases, out-of-pocket health expenditures are expected to increase. The elderly are also likely to find physician excess charges and uncovered pharmaceutical expenses rising. These trends may be exacerbated if current projections of future Medicare deficits and of elderly population growth generate predicted reductions in some Medicare coverage.

Since 1965, Americans over age 65 have been a unique group in terms of health insurance coverage. They have enjoyed almost universal coverage based solely on age. Medicare coverage approximately doubled from 1967 to 1996, when it encompassed 38 million persons (Health Care Financing Administration, 1997). The Medicare population is projected to increase an average of 2 percent a year for the next 20 years. As the largest public payer for personal health care expenditures, Medicare is not only the largest payer for each of the acute care services covered, but it has also covered increasingly large shares of the spending on each. In 1995, Medicare covered 21 percent of total health care expenditures, including 20 percent of physician services and 32 percent of hospital care. Growth in hospital admissions per 1,000 population was generated exclusively by elderly admissions (Levit et al., 1996). For the last 15 years, Medicare costs have grown at an average annual rate of 11 percent (Gramm, 1997). Further, 10 percent of Medicare beneficiaries account for 70 percent of program expenditures (Kaiser Family Foundation, 1995).

In addition to nearly universal Medicare coverage, 89 percent of the elderly have some sort of supplemental insurance. One-third receive health insurance coverage from a former employer, 37 percent buy supplemental (Medigap) insurance, 12 percent are covered by Medicaid,[1] and a small group has employer plus individual or other coverage. Thus, only the remaining 11 percent of the elderly are without any supplemental coverage (Kaiser Family Foundation, 1995). Yet despite extensive third-party health coverage, the out-of-pocket health care costs of those age 65 and over continue to increase. Medicare finances only about 45 percent of all health care spending on the elderly, as cost sharing is relatively high and Medicare does not cover outpatient prescriptions or most long-term care. Further, the typical Medigap policy generally does not cover services that are left uncovered by Medicare (e.g., prescriptions). Most elderly incur out-of-pocket charges for pharmaceuticals, vision and dental care, deductibles, co-payments, and provider charges in excess of those allowed (balance billing).

Older Americans allocated roughly 12 percent of their total spending to health care in 1995 (see Table 2.5). Despite the massive expenditures made by Medicare, elderly families allocate the same proportion of out-of-pocket dollars to private health insurance as in the pre-Medicare era (Families USA Foundation, 1992). Between 1970 and 1995, out-of-pocket health care costs of the elderly rose 72 percent ("A Warning Sign," 1996). Aged persons, who account for over 35 percent of all health care expenditures, had out-of-pocket health expenses over $90 billion in 1995. On average, Medicare beneficiaries spent $2,750 out-of-pocket for health care services and health insurance premiums in 1995 (Kaiser Family Foundation, 1995), compared to $1,697 in 1988 (Piacentini and Cerino, 1990).

This chapter presents analyses of health care expenditures of the elderly, with emphasis on the impact of public and private third-party payments on their out-of-pocket health care spending. The next section presents a brief overview of previous studies of out-of-pocket health expenditures. Then, we offer detailed discussion of three of our empirical studies of the determinants of out-of-pocket health spending by elderly households, followed by our conclusions and the policy implications of our findings.

OUT-OF-POCKET HEALTH EXPENDITURES

The findings of previous studies of health care expenditures are fairly consistent. There is adequate empirical evidence to demonstrate that the net price paid out-of-pocket is a determinant of the quantity of services purchased for at least some health care utilization. Thus, some health care spending has the generally expected price characteristics of economic demand (Zweifel, 1990). The Rand National Health Insurance Experiment provided significant contributions to understanding the impacts of out-of-pocket payments on health care decision making. This unique study demonstrated that families who were assigned to a co-insurance plan had 25 percent lower medical expenditures than those receiving free care (Newhouse et al., 1981). A further finding was that physician-related cost sharing had a larger effect on demand reduction than hospital-related cost sharing (Smeeding and Straub, 1987).

Other studies have related out-of-pocket payments to use of health care, with some analyses emphasizing the relationship of medical symptoms to spending. Patients required to make co-payments for care are more likely to have serious medical symptoms (Shapiro, Ware, and Sherbourne, 1986). Shapiro and colleagues (1989) concluded that co-payments over $15 were associated with decreased use of care for serious as well as minor symptoms, and the likelihood of seeking care for both major and minor medical symptoms declined as out-of-pocket payments increased. In a study of high-cost users of medical care, Garfinkel, Riley, and Iannacchione (1988) found that insurance cost sharing increased out-of-pocket medical spending but limited the number of households that incurred high out-of-pocket costs. They also found that nonelderly persons paid 25 percent of all incurred costs, with a much lower share for high-cost users, and that the same pattern held for those over age 65.

Health cost growth is unlikely to be restrained solely by supply side cost-containment strategies (Schneider and Guralnik, 1990). Thus, cost-containment policies are most likely to emphasize the demand side, including increased cost sharing to affect economic incentives and greater out-of-pocket health payments. Increased cost sharing is likely to have the heaviest impact on those who are older and sicker and least able to afford it. Out-of-pocket health costs have the greatest impact on poor and near-poor elderly. In particular, those with only Medicare insurance are the least able to afford increased out-of-pocket costs. For the elderly with income less than $5,000, out-of-pocket costs are 21 percent of income, declining to only 2 percent for those with income over $30,000 (Smeeding and Straub, 1987).

Numerous expenditure studies using CE Survey data include health care as one of the budget categories. Housing and medical care have considerably higher relative weights (budget shares) for older households, compared to households of all ages (Ruffin, 1989). The retired (in 1972) allocated a larger part of an increase in income to medical care, shelter, and gifts and contributions than to other budget items (McConnel and Deljavan, 1983). In particular, for retirees, 5 percent of an additional dollar of income was absorbed by direct (out-of-pocket) medical expenses, whereas only 1 percent of an additional income dollar was allocated to health care by nonretirees. Harrison (1986) found that the 65 to 74 age group spent over 8 percent of total expenditures on health care, while the 75 and over age group spent more than 13 percent on health. Moehrle (1990) found that older, nonworking households spend more on health care than those working, regardless of income level. These findings may relate to the nonworking elderly having less private insurance coverage and more health problems than the working elderly.

EMPIRICAL ANALYSES—DATA AND METHODOLOGY

As the U.S. population continues to age and health costs escalate, detailed information on household health spending is needed for both national and state health policy planning. Analysis of out-of-pocket health expenditures is also relevant for business decision making as employment costs of health insurance and retiree coverage increase. Despite the importance of data on household health spending, relatively few studies have provided detailed examinations of out-of-pocket health spending. We extend previous research with three studies of out-of-pocket health care expenditures, using the explanatory variables of permanent income, age, race, assets, insurance coverage, housing tenure, education level, and family size. First, we analyze health expenditures, comparing elderly and nonelderly households by income level. We next examine change over the decade of the 1980s in out-of-pocket health spending by elderly households. Third, we analyze the impact of Medigap insurance on out-of-pocket health expenditures, again examining change over the 1980s.

Data

Consumer Expenditure (CE) Interview Survey data are used in these three studies. The sample criteria, presented in Chapter 1, include only complete income reporters, with after-tax income greater than zero and living independently. Elderly households are determined by having a respondent (reference person) or spouse age 65 or over, because Medicare eligibility begins on the first day of the month of the sixty-fifth birthday (Omenn, 1990). The nonelderly comparison group includes only households with no older persons in residence.

Due to the unique nature of health care spending, several additional criteria are imposed to accurately encompass household out-of-pocket spending. First, military households or welfare (AFDC or SSI) recipients are excluded, as persons in both of these groups receive health care with no or minimal out-of-pocket charges. Second, only consumer units with four quarters of data are included, so recorded data for each household is summed across four quarters to determine annual expenditures. This accounts for the random and unplanned nature of many health expenditures. It also allows us to largely avoid the potential problems of annualizing quarterly data for expenditures that are likely to vary significantly across the year and might be zero in any given quarter.

Third, in the CE Survey, out-of-pocket health expenditures include spending on insurance and direct payments for medical goods and services as well as any reimbursements received from insurance companies for payments made in the past (Acs and Sabelhaus, 1995). Since insurance-reimbursed amounts are included as negative medical care expenditures in the CE Interview Survey, reimbursements by third-party payers are deducted from the household expenditures by category (Branch, 1987). Households are excluded from the samples if their insurance reimbursements are $2,000 or more greater than their out-of-pocket health expenditures, because these refunds may be received months after the costs are incurred.

For elderly persons, who are virtually all covered by Medicare, the insurance coverage dummy variable reflects only supplemental insurance coverage. This variable is not available directly from the data base and is estimated from two indicators: insurance payments and any refunds for medical expenses. Because the CE Survey data base includes only out-of-pocket payments, it does not indicate health insurance premiums paid fully by an employer. Thus, a limited number of households that have employer-provided health insurance but no health care refunds during the study period may be incorrectly classified as uninsured.

While the CE Survey data base is a major source for out-of-pocket expenditure data, it does not contain any health status indicators. To compensate for the lack of health status variables, we assume the effects of health status will be proxied by age (Long, Settle, and Link, 1982). Institutionalized persons in long-term care facilities are not included in the CE Survey data base; however, those with acute care hospitalizations are included, and this status is reflected in hospital expenditures.

In the first empirical analysis, health expenditure data are pooled for the period 1986 to 1988 to increase the sample number of households meeting our criteria. In the following two analyses, data are pooled for each of two comparison periods, with 1989–1990 being the focus period and 1980–1981 the comparison period. As in Chapter 5, data for these pooled years are referred to as 1980 or 1990 data to simplify our presentation. To facilitate comparisons, all monetary variables are expressed in constant 1990 dollars, using the Consumer Price Index (CPI) to inflate 1980–1981 values. Therefore, all growth indicated is relative to the general price level, after accounting for inflation. Using the 1982–1984 CPI base year, the CPI value is 90.9 for 1981 and 133.8 for 1990.

Methodology

In the three analyses of out-of-pocket health expenditures, we initially use descriptive statistics to compare mean out-of-pocket expenditures on categories of health care by different sample groups (elderly and nonelderly by income level or time period or those with and without Medigap insurance), to determine if their mean expenditures or mean budget shares are different. In addition, we conduct regression analyses to determine the relationships between out-of-pocket health expenditures and the economic and demographic characteristics of elderly households.

As in Chapter 5, we use two-stage least squares regression analysis to estimate the effects of demographic and economic variables on out-of-pocket health expenditures for elderly households and comparison groups. The results of the second-stage regressions indicate how out-of-pocket health expenditures depend on demographic and economic variables for the different groups of households. The β coefficient for each independent variable measures its impact on a dependent variable category of out-of-pocket health spending. The second-stage models differ slightly among the three studies to allow analysis and comparison of different targeted groups and health expenditure categories. These models are specified as:

MODEL 1—to compare differentials between elderly and nonelderly health expenditures:

$$H_i = \alpha_1 + \beta_1 I_i + \beta_2 Age_i + \beta_3 Race_i + \beta_4 Assets_i + \beta_5 Ins_i$$
$$+ \beta_6 Home_i + \beta_7 Education_i + \beta_8 Size_i + u_i$$

where

H_i = ln (annual out-of-pocket health expenditure of household i)

I_i = ln (total expenditure estimate from stage 1 of household i)

Age_i = ln (age of reference person of household i)

$Race_i$ = 1 if household i is white; 0 if non-white

$Assets_i$ = ln (net financial asset value of household i)

Ins_i = 1 if household i has health insurance; 0 if not

$Home_i$ = 1 if household i owns their home; 0 if rents

$Education_i$ = ln (years of schooling of reference person i)

$Size_i$ = ln (number of persons in household i)

u_i is normally distributed disturbance term.

MODEL 2—to compare elderly health expenditures over the 1980s:

$$H_i = \alpha + \beta_1 I_i + \beta_2 Age_i + \beta_3 Size_i + \beta_4 Home_i + \beta_5 Race_i$$
$$+ \beta_6 Education_i + \beta_7 Ins_i + u_i$$

where

H_i = ln (annual out-of-pocket health expenditure of household i)

I_i = ln (total expenditure estimate from stage 1 of household i)

Age_i = ln (age of reference person of household i)

$Size_i$ = ln (number of persons in household i)

$Home_i$ = 1 if household i owns their home; 0 if rents

$Race_i$ = 1 if household i is white; 0 if non-white

$Education_i$ = ln (years of schooling of reference person i)

Ins_i = 1 if household i has insurance, 0 if not (omitted in the case of health insurance as the dependent variable)

u_i is normally distributed disturbance term.

MODEL 3—to compare the impact of Medigap insurance on elderly health expenditures over the 1980s:

$$H_i = \alpha_1 + \beta_1 I_i + \beta_2 Age_i + \beta_3 Race_i + \beta_4 Ins_i + \beta_5 Home_i + \beta_6 Couple_i + u_i$$

where

H_i = ln (annual out-of-pocket health expenditure of household i)

I_i = ln (total expenditure estimate from stage 1 of household i)

Age_i = ln (age of reference person of household i)

$Race_i$ = 1 if white; 0 if non-white

Ins_i = 1 if household i has Medigap insurance, 0 if not

$Home_i$ = 1 if household i owns their home; 0 if rents

$Couple_i$ = 1 if household i is a couple; 0 if single

u_i is normally distributed disturbance term.

Since both the permanent income variable and the dependent variables are in logged form in these models, the permanent income parameters provide estimates of income elasticities of the dependent variables.

Detailed information on household health care spending is crucial to health policy planning. Changes in health policy will be efficient and equitable only if they are grounded in accurate empirical information. While business and government health spending data are available, few previous studies have examined out-of-pocket health expenditures, and those have largely been descriptive. We use the three models developed above for empirical analyses of health expenditures by households of different ages and income levels, and over time.

ELDERLY AND NONELDERLY HEALTH EXPENDITURES: EMPIRICAL STUDY I

This section provides detailed and extensive analysis of out-of-pocket health expenditures. Regression analysis is used to compare elderly and nonelderly households by income level to determine whether higher-income elderly and nonelderly spend differently for health care than lower-income households. The two broad research questions examined are: How do out-of-pocket expenditures of elderly households differ from those of the nonelderly, and what socioeconomic factors are important in determining these differences? Second, how do out-of-pocket health expenditures of higher-income elderly and nonelderly differ from those of lower-income households, and what are the important determinants of these differences? This study was published in *The Gerontologist*.[2]

Sample Characteristics

The two CE Interview Survey samples, with pooled data for 1986 to 1988, are households with a reference person or spouse aged 65 and over and households without an elderly person. Both age categories were split at the median after-tax income ($22,346) of the entire sample to determine lower- and higher-income groups. This approach is based on an earlier study (Cafferata, 1984) in which high-income families were defined as having income at least four times the poverty threshold. The 1987 poverty threshold for elderly households was $5,447 and for nonelderly was $5,909. Thus, the sample median income falls between four times the elderly poverty level ($21,788) and four times the nonelderly poverty level ($23,636). The data indicate that this median income corresponds closely to the point at which both elderly and nonelderly households have income that exceeds current expenditures (i.e., begin to have positive savings). This process yields unequal subgroups, as the higher-income group is almost 50 percent larger than the lower-income group for the nonelderly, whereas for the elderly the higher-income group is only one-fourth as large as the lower-income group.

Although average after-tax income levels of both elderly income groups ($10,119 and $38,603) are lower than for the nonelderly ($12,920 and $42,753), financial assets are considerably greater for the elderly. Average assets of the higher-income elderly ($49,400) are almost four times those of the lower-income elderly ($13,381), while assets of the higher-income nonelderly ($15,920) are about three times those of the lower-income nonelderly ($5,277). Home ownership shows less variation among the elderly than the nonelderly, with 90 percent of higher-income and 73 percent of lower-income elderly being home owners, compared to 87 percent and 54 percent for the comparable nonelderly groups.

Age of the reference person has greater variation for the elderly than the nonelderly. While lower-income elderly average 74 years, the higher-income average is 70; for the nonelderly, the averages are 41 and 42 years. Both nonelderly groups have substantially higher levels of education than the comparable elderly groups, reflecting a major social trend toward higher education levels.

Findings

Table 6.1 presents the mean out-of-pocket health expenditures for the detailed CE categories for elderly and nonelderly households by lower and higher income levels. Overall, households with higher income have substantially greater out-of-pocket insurance and medical care expenditures than those with lower income, and the elderly spend almost twice as much on health as the nonelderly in comparable income groups. However, comparing by income level, the elderly spend less on eyewear than the nonelderly, and on hospital rooms and nonphysician practitioners, probably due to Medicare coverage. The largest differentials between elderly and nonelderly health spending are for insurance and prescription drugs not covered by Medicare.

Out-of-pocket health expenditure budget shares reveal substantial differences between the income and age groups. Health spending takes a much higher share of total expenditures (14 percent) for elderly with lower incomes than for those with higher incomes (8 percent). This differential is much less for the nonelderly (5 percent compared with 4 percent).

Regression Results

Table 6.2 presents the second-stage regression results for out-of-pocket health care expenditures exclusive of medical insurance payments, which are excluded since health insurance is used as an independent dummy variable. The regression model is run for seven groups: the entire sample, the two age groups, and by higher and lower income for each age group.

To determine if the expenditure functions for each group are different (i.e., if the coefficients differ) we conducted five Chow tests. First, we find that elderly and nonelderly do have significantly different expenditure functions (Chow = 3.4). Second, we find that within the nonelderly, the low-income group has a different expenditure function than the high-income group (Chow = 5.68). Third, within the elderly, the low-income group has a different expenditure function than the high-income group (Chow = 1.64). Fourth, we also find that within the low-income group, the elderly and nonelderly differ (Chow = 2.32). Fifth, we find that within the high-income group, the nonelderly and elderly do not have significantly different expenditure functions (Chow = 1.37). In general, we find that there are many significant differences. We focus particularly on the differences in the permanent income parameter because it provides a measure of the income elasticity of expenditure on health care for each group. It indicates the percentage change in spending on health care for a 1 percent change in income. For example, a

Table 6.1
Mean Out-of-Pocket Health Expenditures of Nonelderly and Elderly Households: 1986–1988

Health Expenditures	Nonelderly		Elderly	
	Lower Income[a]	Higher Income	Lower Income	Higher Income
Health Insurance	$307	$403	$678	$927
Commercial	143	205	112	207
Blue Cross	89	102	161	184
HMO Plans	31	55	32	87
Medicare	10	3	249	279
Other Insurance	33	38	124	169
Drugs & Medical Supplies	142	205	344	419
Prescription Drugs	104	128	291	327
Eyeglasses/Contacts	35	68	31	64
Medical Equipment	1	3	11	10
Convalescent Med. Equip.	1	5	9	16
Rental Equipment	1	1	2	2
Medical Services	394	668	580	762
Institutional	76	95	210	73
Hospital Room	43	56	36	38
Hospital Ancillary	32	38	32	24
Nursing Home	1	1	142	11
Physician Services	149	242	171	244
Other	169	331	200	445
Dental Services	106	231	106	296
Eyecare Services	17	27	31	56
Non-physician Practitioner	16	29	15	27
Lab Tests & X-rays	17	29	27	41
Nursing Services	2	3	8	11
Other Services	10	12	13	16
Total	$843	$1,276	$1,602	$2,107

[a] Income group is determined by median income based on reported after-tax income for entire sample ($22,346).

Source: R. M. Rubin and K. Koelln, 1993, Out-of-pocket health expenditure differentials between elderly and non-elderly households, *The Gerontologist*, 33(5): 595–602. Reprinted by permission of The Gerontological Society of America.

1 percent increase in income motivates a 2.17 percent increase in lower-income elderly spending on total health care, but for lower-income nonelderly households, health expenditure would increase only 1.15 percent in response to a 1 percent increase in income. Based on the

Table 6.2
Out-of-Pocket Health Expenditure Regression Results, Comparing Nonelderly and Elderly: 1986–1988

Variables	All	Non elderly	Elderly	Low Income Non elderly	Low Income Elderly	High Income Non elderly	High Income Elderly
Constant	-6.19 *	-6.15 *	-21.47 *	-10.55 *	-35.74 *	-2.66 *	-3.05
Log of Permanent Income	0.64 *	0.74 *	1.19 *	1.15 *	2.17 *	0.46 *	0.16
Log of Age (reference)	1.04 *	0.76 *	3.42 *	0.90 *	4.70 *	0.60 *	1.50
Race (reference)	0.78 *	0.71 *	0.79 *	0.78 *	0.56 *	0.55 *	0.76 *
Log of Assets	0.03 *	0.03 *	0.01	0.03 *	-0.01	0.03 *	0.02
Insurance	0.73 *	0.69 *	1.25 *	0.87 *	1.59 *	0.51 *	0.33
Housing Tenure	-0.36 *	-0.33 *	-0.48 *	-0.36 *	-0.49 *	-0.19 *	0.10
Log of Education	0.15 *	0.15 *	-0.05	0.05	-0.24	0.22 *	0.13
Log of Family Size	0.51 *	0.53 *	0.24	0.42 *	-0.26	0.58	0.32
R^2	0.22	0.23	0.19	0.22	0.19	0.12	0.04
F-Value	230.54	188.64	47.21	72.92	36.72	50.19	1.74
Chow Tests:							
Elderly vs. Nonelderly	3.40 *						
Low income vs. high income		5.68 *	1.64 *				
Elderly vs. nonelderly				2.32 *		1.37	

*Statistically significant at p<0.10.

Source: R. M. Rubin and K. Koelln, 1993, Out-of-pocket health expenditure differentials between elderly and non-elderly households, *The Gerontologist*, 33(5): 595–602. Reprinted by permission of The Gerontological Society of America.

permanent income coefficient for both lower income age groups, medical goods and services would be classified as "luxuries," and this is especially the case for the elderly. In contrast, the data indicate that higher-income groups allocate a decreasing share of an increase in income to medical care, which has an income elasticity less than one. Thus, for higher-income households, medical care fits the economic definition of a "necessity."

Health insurance is purchased to reduce the risk of out-of-pocket health expenditures, so a negative insurance parameter would a priori be expected. However, we find a positive and significant insurance parameter for all groups, except the higher-income elderly for whom it is positive but not significant. Thus, our regression results indicate that households with health insurance have increased spending on co-payments, deductibles, and noncovered medical care.[3] This may reflect either that there is increased demand by those with insurance (termed moral hazard) or that households purchase health insurance when they anticipate needing it (termed adverse selection).

Home ownership is negatively related to expenditures on health care goods and services for all groups except higher-income elderly. In contrast, the financial assets parameter is generally positive and a significant determinant of out-of-pocket health expenditures for all households and the nonelderly, but not for the elderly. The lack of significance of the assets parameter for the elderly may indicate that these assets are wiped out by large health expenditures or that they are divested when ill health is apparent. Alternately, it may simply reflect the widespread use of Medigap coverage by the elderly regardless of wealth holdings. The findings on home ownership and financial assets may be related by the possibility that the elderly in poorer health are unable to maintain independent homes and also spend more on health care.

Age is significant and positive for all households, except higher-income elderly. Race is significant and positive for all household categories, indicating that white households spend more out-of-pocket on medical care. Education level is somewhat less important as a health expenditure determinant than the other variables, and it has the least impact among older persons. Family size is a less important factor for elderly households than for nonelderly, probably because they encompass a smaller size range. Overall, among the sociodemographic variables, race and housing tenure are significant determinants of health spending for both age groups. In contrast, family size, assets, and education are significant only for nonelderly households.

HEALTH EXPENDITURE CHANGE OVER THE 1980s:
EMPIRICAL STUDY II

This section compares out-of-pocket health expenditures of elderly and nonelderly households over the 1980s. We focus on differences in household health expenditure patterns attributable to universal insurance coverage rather than differences caused by health problems of aging. While elderly households generally have more insurance coverage and also incur higher health costs, their increases in out-of-pocket expenditures over the 1980s were mainly for insurance premiums rather than medical goods and services. Medicare is shown to have promoted equity in elderly health spending during the decade, which has strong implications for the potential distributional equity of national health insurance programs. This research was published in the *Journal of Gerontology: Social Sciences*.[4]

Sample Characteristics

Elderly and nonelderly samples are studied for 1980 and 1990 to analyze health expenditure change by age group over the decade. Overall, the elderly households are: smaller, averaging 1.7 persons compared with 3 nonelderly persons in 1980 and 2.9 in 1990; more likely to be white (92 percent compared with 88 percent of nonelderly); more likely to be home owners (79 percent compared with 72 percent of nonelderly in 1990); but with lower levels of education than the nonelderly.

Consistent with the samples in the first study discussed above, elderly households have substantially lower after-tax income and higher levels of financial assets in both time periods. Real average income (in constant 1990 dollars) increased over seven thousand dollars for nonelderly and over four thousand for elderly households over the decade. However, the income of older households was roughly half that of nonelderly households in both 1980 ($14,803 compared to $27,725) and 1990 ($19,102 compared to $34,784). In contrast, average financial assets of the elderly ($12,973 in 1980 and $25,560 in 1990) grew relatively and absolutely more than those of nonelderly ($7,433 in 1980 and $12,313 in 1990).

Findings

Table 6.3 shows mean out-of-pocket health expenditures in constant 1990 dollars for the four groups (elderly and nonelderly for 1980 and 1990) and the percentage change between 1980 and 1990.[5] While average

Table 6.3
Mean Out-of-Pocket Health Expenditures of Nonelderly and Elderly
Households: 1980 and 1990 (1990 Dollars)

Mean Out-of-Pocket Health Expenditures	Nonelderly			Elderly		
	1980	1990	% Change	1980	1990	% Change
Health Insurance	$313	$534	71	$519	$1071	106
Commercial	127	224	77	123	190	54
Blue Cross	129	137	6	162	253	56
HMO Plans	17	91	422	9	55	484
Medicare	10	22	117	167	374	125
Other Insurance	29	60	103	57	200	248
Drugs & Medical Supplies	162	211	30	316	479	52
Prescription Drugs	117	142	22	264	400	52
Eyeglasses/Contacts	38	60	56	32	50	58
Medical Equipment	7	9	20	21	29	40
Medical Services	583	625	7	731	701	-4
Institutional	77	117	52	119	149	26
Hospital Room	47	46	-2	65	57	-12
Hospital Ancillary	22	53	140	43	43	0
Nursing Home	7	17	135	11	49	338
Physician Services	213	214	1	247	224	-10
Other	294	294	0	364	327	-10
Dental Services	202	197	-3	145	197	35
Eyecare Services	35	27	-24	52	41	-20
Non-physician Practice	23	27	21	25	18	-30
Lab Tests & X-rays	24	28	17	31	32	4
Nursing Services	4	6	47	97	30	-70
Other Services	7	10	50	14	10	-30
Total	1058	1369	29	1566	2251	44

Source: R. M. Rubin, K. Koelln, and R. K. Speas, Jr., 1995, Out-of-pocket health expenditures by elderly households: Change over the 1980s, *Journal of Gerontology*, 50B(5): S291–S300. Reprinted by permission of The Gerontological Society of America.

total out-of-pocket health expenditures increased for both age groups between 1980 and 1990, the percentage increase is considerably larger for older households (44 percent) than for those without older members (29 percent). Average expenditures in a limited number of health categories actually decreased over the decade. In particular, spending for eyecare declined at least 20 percent for both age groups, probably reflecting increased competition in the eyecare industry. For the elderly, there were also decreases in mean spending for hospital rooms, physician services, nonphysician practice, nursing services, and other services. The 70 percent decline in mean expenditure for nursing services is not due to a change in the percent reporting these expenditures, and is, therefore, probably due to increased Medicare coverage of this health care service.

Of the broad CE categories, health insurance shows the largest increase over the period (106 percent for elderly households and 71 percent for nonelderly). For the elderly, Medicare premium payments show a 125 percent increase over the decade. This growth is related to government efforts to control its share of program costs by shifting costs to users. Other insurance includes out-of-pocket payments for insurance policies that are not in any of the four specific categories and payments for commercial Medicare supplements (Medigap policies), dental insurance, and other health insurance (U.S. Department of Labor, 1991a). Our finding of the doubling of elderly spending for health insurance confirms earlier research that consumer resources have shifted from direct out-of-pocket health payments to those handled by third-party payers (Levit, Freeland, and Waldo, 1990).

In 1990, the elderly spent almost three times as much on prescription drugs as nonelderly purchasers, reflecting both their greater usage of prescriptions and noncoverage by Medicare. In contrast, for medical services, which are generally covered by Medicare, elderly households incurred only 12 percent higher out-of-pocket costs than nonelderly households in 1990. The largest percentage increase in health care expenditures occurred for the elderly for nursing home services, despite the fact that the CE Survey does not include those institutionalized and only 1 to 2 percent of households reported nursing home expenses (explaining the very small average amount spent).

Regression Results

Regression analyses of expenditure patterns on health care by household group use the two-stage least squares model described above. For the elderly and nonelderly household groups in each time period, the model is run on four dependent variables: total out-of-pocket health care expenditures (exclusive of insurance premiums), expenditures on prescription drugs and medical supplies, expenditures on medical services, and expenditures on health insurance. The explanatory variables are various socioeconomic variables, health insurance (except when health insurance expenditure is the dependent variable), and the first-stage estimated permanent income.

The regression results are reported in Table 6.4. The permanent income parameter is positive and highly significant for the model of total health expenditures for nonelderly households in both time periods, and significant for elderly households for 1980 but not for 1990. It is much smaller for elderly households than for nonelderly. Further, the nonsignificant permanent income parameter for the elderly in 1990 indicates that income is not a major determinant of their health care spending. This parameter is positive and highly significant for medical services for all household groups in both time periods. Further, medical services is a luxury good in 1980 for both groups. For prescription drugs, the permanent income parameter is significantly different from zero only for nonelderly households; for health insurance, it is highly significant for nonelderly households in 1990 and significant for elderly households in both 1980 and 1990. The Chow statistic for change over time for the elderly for health insurance is very large, indicating the significant change in their demand for health insurance. Further, the income elasticity for health insurance has declined, indicating the strong demand for health insurance across all income classes.

Age is an important explanatory variable in all cases, except for prescription drugs for elderly households in 1980. It is positive, indicating increased health care spending with aging, particularly for elderly who have age elasticities greater than one. The race variable is highly significant for nonelderly households (except for health insurance), indicating that whites spend more on health care. White elderly spend more on health insurance and prescription drugs and medical supplies in 1990 than blacks. Home ownership is a positive and more important determinant of health spending for elderly households in 1990 than in 1980. The education parameter is not significant for elderly households. Family size is significant, as expected, in all cases for total health expenditures and for prescription drugs. It is not significant for elderly households for medical services in either period nor for health insurance in 1980.

Previous studies (Manning et al., 1987; Shapiro et al., 1989; Rubin and Koelln, 1993) found that persons with third-party coverage consume relatively more medical care (i.e., a moral hazard exists), and our data extend these findings. The insurance variable in Table 6.4 is positive and highly significant for all models in the three categories where it is used. However, our findings have a slightly different interpretation than the usual moral hazard problem, where consumers use more health care once thay have paid a fixed insurance premium. The households in our study are spend-

Table 6.4
Out-of-Pocket Health Expenditure Regression Results: 1980 and 1990

	Nonelderly		Elderly	
Variables	**1980**	**1990**	**1980**	**1990**
Total Spending on Health Goods & Services (Exclusive of Ins. Premiums)				
Constant	-7.26 *	-6.00 *	-4.08	-2.94
Ln Permanent Income	0.82 *	0.55 *	0.48 *	0.14
Ln Age (reference)	0.90 *	1.07 *	1.18 *	1.76 *
Race (reference)	0.68 *	0.72 *	0.33	0.17
Insurance	0.54 *	0.64 *	0.62 *	0.44 *
Housing Tenure	0.11	0.37 *	-0.02	0.19 *
Ln Education	0.03	0.28 *	-0.10	0.10
Ln Family Size	0.35 *	0.59 *	0.51 *	0.66 *
R^2	0.13	0.16	0.14	0.16
F-value	67.29 *	101.24 *	18.90 *	28.73 *
Chow Nonelderly/Elderly	26.62 *	30.50 *		
Chow Over Time	6.00 *		2.17 *	
Prescription Drugs and Medical Supplies				
Constant	-6.48 *	-5.98 *	1.59	-2.68
Ln Permanent Income	0.53 *	0.40 *	-0.40	-0.12
Ln Age (reference)	0.98 *	1.04 *	1.15	1.58 *
Race (reference)	0.50 *	0.74 *	0.27	0.48 *
Insurance	0.63 *	0.84 *	1.15 *	1.12 *
Housing Tenure	0.16	0.36 *	0.05	0.14
Ln Education	0.02	0.08	0.21	0.14
Ln Family Size	0.36 *	0.48 *	1.30 *	1.22 *
R^2	0.11	0.13	0.09	0.10
F-value	53.89 *	77.27 *	11.63 *	16.61 *
Chow Nonelderly/Elderly	17.33 *	8.95 *		
Chow Over Time	2.54 *		0.00	

ing more out-of-pocket (exclusive of premiums) on health care than households without insurance.

The Chow tests used to determine if the differences in the dependent variable coefficients are statistically significant across sample groups are shown in Table 6.4. The Chow statistics relating the two age groups indicate that the age group models are significantly different in the four

Table 6.4 (*continued*)

Variables	Nonelderly		Elderly	
	1980	1990	1980	1990
Medical Services				
Constant	-11.51 *	-8.30 *	-16.48 *	-13.26 *
Ln Permanent Income	1.39 *	0.94 *	1.31 *	0.93 *
Ln Age (reference)	0.38 *	0.42 *	1.79 *	1.76 *
Race (reference)	0.72 *	0.75 *	0.55 *	0.21
Insurance	0.55 *	0.70 *	1.21 *	0.98 *
Housing Tenure	0.01	0.39 *	0.00	0.59 *
Ln Education	-0.08	0.27 *	-0.13	0.23
Ln Family Size	0.31 *	0.55 *	0.26	0.35
R^2	0.12	0.16	0.14	0.15
F-value	58.14 *	96.12 *	18.06 *	25.96 *
Chow Nonelderly/Elderly	4.55 *	6.02 *		
Chow Over Time	4.46 *		3.32 *	
Health Insurance				
Constant	-2.22	-8.13 *	-4.32	-3.27
Ln Permanent Income	-0.22	0.56 *	0.53 *	0.22 *
Ln Age (reference)	1.84 *	1.56 *	1.05 *	1.64 *
Race (reference)	0.06	0.22	0.43 *	0.45 *
Insurance				
Housing Tenure	0.50 *	0.33 *	0.29 *	0.21 *
Ln Education	0.45 *	0.09	-0.04	-0.03
Ln Family Size	0.25	0.15	0.10	0.48 *
R^2	0.05	0.04	0.06	0.11
F-value	29.61 *	27.00 *	8.67 *	21.84 *
Chow Nonelderly/Elderly	44.30 *	33.78 *		
Chow Over Time	8.87 *		32.70 *	

* Statistically significant at $p < 0.10$

Source: R. M. Rubin, K. Koelln, and R. K. Speas, Jr., 1995, Out-of-pocket health expenditures by elderly households: Change over the 1980s, *Journal of Gerontology*, 50B(5): S291–S300. Reprinted by permission of The Gerontological Society of America.

models analyzed for both time periods. The Chow over-time statistics indicate that the models are significantly different for the two time periods, except for prescription drugs and medical supplies for elderly households.

THE IMPACT OF MEDIGAP INSURANCE ON HEALTH EXPENDITURES OVER THE 1980s: EMPIRICAL STUDY III

This section analyzes elderly health expenditure patterns and health financing and compares the effects of Medigap insurance[6] on out-of-pocket spending over the past decade. This research, with national health policy implications, is based on a study published in the *Journal of Economics and Finance.*[7]

Sample Characteristics

The CE samples for 1980 (n = 742) and 1990 (n = 957) are drawn in accordance with the criteria detailed above. These are first separated into elderly singles and couples, with each size household then disaggregated into "Medicare Only" and "Medigap" categories, determined by the out-of-pocket payment of insurance premiums.[8] This results in four sample groups for each time period. The share of sample households with Medigap insurance increased over time, from 63 percent to 70 percent for singles and from 71 percent to 78 percent for couples.

The demographic profiles of the samples present generally expected characteristics. The average reference person's age of couples (72) is slightly lower than average age of singles (75). Average education levels increased over time, most notably for those with Medicare Only. For single elderly with Medigap insurance, home ownership increased over the 1980s (from 62 to 68 percent), but not for those with Medicare Only. In contrast, for couples, home ownership increased for the Medicare Only groups (from 79 to 91 percent), but not for those with Medigap. In general, Medigap insurance holders are more highly educated and more likely to be white and home owners.

The growth in real (constant dollar) income and financial assets over the 1980s is noteworthy. Real after-tax income increased relatively more for elderly households with only Medicare coverage, and particularly for couples. After-tax income increased 61 percent for couples with Medicare Only coverage, compared to just 16 percent for couples with Medigap; while it grew 51 percent for singles with Medicare, compared to 42 percent for those with Medigap. The finding that average income of couples with Medicare Only exceeds the income of those with Medigap policies in 1990 was unexpected. It may be that those with poor health and lower income are more likely to purchase additional insurance (i.e., adverse selection) or, possibly, some retirees with fully employer-paid health insurance are classified as Medicare Only.

The growth of constant dollar financial assets (exclusive of housing equity) among these households is even more notable than income growth. Assets increased 84 percent for singles with Medicare Only and 89 percent for singles with Medigap; however, financial assets more than tripled for couples with Medicare Only and more than doubled for those with Medigap. Overall, elderly households appear to be substantially better off at the end of the decade.

Findings

Table 6.5 shows 1980 and 1990 mean out-of-pocket expenditures on categories of health care by singles and couples with Medicare Only and with Medigap policies, and the percentage change over time. All dollar figures are inflated to constant 1990 dollars, so changes are in real terms. Real expenditures for health insurance increased substantially more than out-of-pocket payments for medical goods and services, particularly for households with Medicare Only. This reflects increases in Medicare premiums, which more than doubled. Our finding of a shift in out-of-pocket health budgets toward increased insurance and away from direct medical payments is consistent with the conclusion of Acs and Sabelhaus (1995) that households confronting higher costs at the point of service eventually purchased more insurance to offset these higher fees during the period 1980 to 1992.

Over the 1980s, real total out-of-pocket health expenditures (Table 6.5) increased for singles and couples with Medigap, but declined 7 percent for couples with Medicare Only, driven by reductions in expenditures on all medical services categories. For single elderly with Medicare Only, out-of-pocket expenditures on physician services increased 27 percent, but physician expenditures declined 26 percent for singles with Medigap insurance, and also declined 12 to 13 percent for couples both with and without Medigap. Direct institutional expenditures changed differently for households with and without Medigap. Institutional spending grew by two-thirds over the decade for both groups of households with Medigap policies, but declined substantially for both groups without Medigap. Overall, real spending on medical care increased substantially more over the decade for those with Medigap insurance.

We also examined out-of-pocket health expenditures as a share of total expenditures for the different groups. Elderly singles with Medigap coverage spent approximately twice as large a share of their total spending on health care as those with only Medicare in both 1980 and 1990. Couples with Medigap also spent about twice as large a budget share on health care as those without Medigap in 1990, but this contrast was not found for couples in 1980.

Table 6.5
Mean Out-of-Pocket Health Expenditures of Elderly Singles and Couples, with and without Medigap Insurance: 1980 and 1990 (1990 Dollars)

Expenditure Categories	Singles						Couples					
	Medicare Only			Medigap			Medicare Only			Medigap		
	1980	1990	% Change	1980	1990	% Change	1980	1990	% Change	1980	1990	% Change
Health Insurance	$121	$276	128	$477	$930	95	$208	$458	120	$873	$1,547	77
Commercial				99	155	57				239	308	29
Blue Cross				183	250	37				286	373	30
HMO Plans				11	46	318				15	77	413
Medicare	121	276	128	127	279	120	208	458	120	213	457	115
Other Insurance				57	201	253				121	331	174
Other Medical	429	459	7	678	807	19	1,760	1,365	-22	1,335	1,614	21
Prescriptions & Supplies	153	173	13	205	347	69	448	531	19	442	641	45
Medical Services	276	286	4	473	460	-3	1,313	834	-36	892	972	9
Institutional	71	29	-59	74	123	66	190	135	-29	139	234	68
Physician Services	92	117	27	177	131	-26	349	307	-12	331	287	-13
Other	112	140	25	222	206	-7	774	392	-49	422	451	7
Total	$549	$735	34	$1,155	$1,738	50	$1,968	$1,823	-7	$2,208	$3,160	43

Source: R. M. Rubin, K. Koelln, and R. K. Speas, etc., 1995, The impact of Medigap insurance on out-of-pocket health insurance by older Americans over the 1980s, *Journal of Economics and Finance*, 19(2): 153–170. Reprinted by permission of the *Journal of Economics and Finance*.

Regression Results

Two-stage regression analysis is used to estimate the effects of demographic and economic variables on out-of-pocket health expenditures for elderly households in 1980 and 1990. For each time period, permanent income is estimated in the first-stage regression. In the second stage, we analyze three categories of out-of-pocket health spending for both time periods using the estimated permanent income and various socioeconomic characteristics as explanatory variables. The presence or absence of Medigap insurance is used as an additional explanatory variable to estimate out-of-pocket expenditures only for health goods and services excluding insurance premiums.

The second-stage regression results for the three dependent variables for both periods are presented in Table 6.6. The three models are: total expenditures on health goods and services including insurance premiums, expenditures on health goods and services excluding insurance premiums,

Table 6.6
Out-of-Pocket Health Expenditure Regression Results Comparing Households with and without Medigap Insurance: 1980 and 1990

Expenditure Category	Health Goods and Services (Including Insur. Premiums)		Health Goods and Services (Excluding Insur. Premiums)		Medical Insurance	
	1980	1990	1980	1990	1980	1990
Constant	-6.20 *	-2.69	-13.40 *	-4.91	-2.20	-1.14
Ln Permanent Income	0.64 *	0.35 *	0.68 *	0.46 *	0.53 *	0.18
Ln Age (reference)	1.48 *	1.38 *	2.69 *	1.09	0.57	1.24
Race (reference)	0.35 *	0.33 *	0.29	0.51 *	0.30 *	0.40
Insurance			1.02 *	0.98 *		
Housing Tenure	0.11	0.16 *	-0.12	0.25 *	0.24 *	0.12
Couple	0.49 *	0.57 *	0.82 *	0.76 *	0.25 *	0.51
F-Value	30.07 *	61.55 *	25.16 *	30.30 *	13.69 *	28.91
R^2	0.17	0.25	0.17	0.16	0.09	0.13
Sample Size	742	957	742	957	742	957

*Statistically significant at $p < 0.10$.

Source: R. M. Rubin, K. Koelln, and R. K. Speas, Jr., 1995, The impact of Medigap insurance on out-of-pocket health expenditures by older Americans over the 1980s, *Journal of Economics and Finance*, 19(2): 153–170. Reprinted by permission of the *Journal of Economics and Finance*.

and medical insurance payments. Although the R^2s appear relatively low, they are consistent with expectations for prediction of health expenditures, which are random and infrequent but tend to be very large when they occur (Newhouse, 1994).

The explanatory variable of Medigap insurance provides a particularly interesting result in the model for health expenditures excluding insurance premiums. The expectation would be that households with Medigap would spend less out-of-pocket on medical goods and services and that the insurance coefficient would be negative, but this is not the case. The coefficient reveals higher medical care expenditures by those with Medigap insurance. Moral hazard and adverse selection are likely the causes of the result. The permanent income parameter is positive and significant in all cases, which is consistent with expectations and shows medical care and health insurance as normal goods, but it is less than one and has declined over time, indicating that medical care has become more of a necessity.

Age is a positive and significant predictor of expenditures on health care including insurance premiums for both time periods, and of 1980 expenditures on health care excluding insurance premiums in 1980, and expenditure on medical insurance in 1990. The results indicate that, in general, white households purchase more medical care and/or pay a higher price for the care they purchase. As expected, increased expenditures were found for couples compared with single households in all models.

CONCLUSIONS AND POLICY IMPLICATIONS

Although detailed information on household health care expenditures is critical for national policy making and household planning, especially for older Americans, previous analyses have been quite limited. The results of the studies reported in this chapter offer insights for health policy development, as the U.S. Medicare model may provide a comparison with alternative national health care policies. Our findings have implications for the ongoing debate on health policy strategies and provide empirical bases for discussion of both efficiency and equity issues in health policy.

We find that income, age, and insurance coverage positively impact out-of-pocket health care expenditures for both elderly and nonelderly households. In addition, we find that effects are much stronger for elderly households.

Our results suggest equity implications for potential health policies, as any national strategy will have to confront considerations of cost containment. One cost solution is to increase deductibles and co-payments for health goods and services. However, even though Medicare enhances equity across some socioeconomic groups, it does not equalize access across income levels. Our findings indicate that medical expenses constitute a "luxury" (in terms of the income elasticity of demand exceeding one) for lower-income elderly households, despite the universality of Medicare for those age 65 and over. The effects of co-payments, deductibles, and coverage limitations influence the much larger share spent on health care by lower-income than higher-income elderly. Thus, if Medicare cost containment is pursued using higher co-payments and deductibles across the eligible population, then increased cost sharing can be expected to impact most heavily on the poorest elderly.

Our results indicate that the elderly relied more heavily on health insurance in 1990 rather than pay directly for health care goods and services. This finding is confirmed by the decline in the income elasticity for spending on medical services and for insurance premiums. As incomes of elderly households increase, their expenditures on health goods and services do not significantly increase (as revealed by the small income elasticity), giving an indication of adequate levels of health care at lower incomes and further emphasizing the importance of Medicare for equity considerations. However, we must be careful in making general statements concerning the effect of income on all elderly households, since we found that income was a significant explanatory variable for the poor elderly. In both 1980 and 1990, the permanent income parameter for the elderly is substantially less than that for nonelderly households.

We find that the real (constant dollar) increases in out-of-pocket medical care expenditures over the last decade were mainly for insurance premiums rather than medical goods and services. This is consistent with findings by Acs and Sabelhaus (1995) for the larger population. In the analysis of the impact of Medigap policies, we find that supplementary insurance does not effectively insulate the elderly from increased out-of-pocket medical expenditures (exclusive of insurance payments). Our results indicate that households with Medigap policies spend over two and a half times as much on health goods and services as those without supplementary coverage.[9] The finding that those with Medigap have higher out-of-pocket expenditures than those with only Medicare occurs over time and across the 1980s. It is highly likely this can be explained by self-selection into the more heavily insured category by those anticipating high health care expenditures. This greater medical care consumption by the elderly with Medigap insurance indicates severe and persistent adverse selection or moral hazard problems.

Medicare provides one model with which we have extensive experience. Empirical analyses of health expenditures of older households emphasize the issues of market failures and thus have important implications for health policy development. The data reveal that adverse selection and moral hazard are likely to be major problems under this model, generating excessive demand and medical care cost inflation. Our findings indicate that the purchase of supplemental insurance tends to increase utilization. However, if co-payments and deductibles are increased to reduce utilization, the poor elderly will be impacted most heavily.

NOTES

1. Low-income elderly covered by Medicare can now have their out-of-pocket expenses covered by Medicaid. Medicaid pays Medicare premiums and other cost-sharing requirements for about 4 million of these "dually eligible" Medicare beneficiaries. In addition, Medicaid also provides benefits not covered by Medicare, such as prescription drugs, for some individuals. Criteria for Medicare beneficiaries to qualify for Medicaid include: eligibility for SSI, sufficiently high medical expenses to "spend down" to Medicaid eligibility levels, or income level below the federal poverty threshold (Kaiser Family Foundation, 1995).

2. Rose M. Rubin and Kenneth Koelln, 1993, Out-of-pocket health expenditure differentials between elderly and non-elderly households, *The Gerontologist*, 33(5): 595–602.

3. This finding is consistent with Rubin and Koelln (1993) for different types of U.S. households.

4. Rose M. Rubin, Kenneth Koelln, and Roger K. Speas, Jr., 1995, Out-of-pocket health expenditures by elderly households: Change over the 1980s, *Journal of Gerontology: Social Sciences*, 50B(5): S291–S300.

5. In the article published in the *Journal of Gerontology: Social Sciences*, in addition to the mean of the entire group, we also present mean data for those reporting health expenditures, because many households report zero for subcategories of health expenditure. This enables analysis of spending growth for those households that incurred out-of-pocket expenditures, rather than growth of the mean for the total group.

6. All supplementary health insurance of the elderly is included as Medigap policies, even though this may include diverse types, such as policies marketed as Medigap plans, indemnity policies, specified disease policies, as well as HMOs and retiree group policies (Garfinkel, Bonito, and McLeroy, 1987).

7. Rose M. Rubin, Kenneth Koelln, and Roger K. Speas, Jr., 1995, The impact of Medigap insurance on out-of-pocket health expenditures by older Americans over the 1980s, *Journal of Economics and Finance*, 19(2): 153–170.

8. The two insurance groups are determined by their expenditure on insurance premiums reported in the CE data. Those with no insurance payments other than Medicare premiums are designated "Medicare Only," and those with Medicare premiums plus some form of supplementary insurance premium payments are in

the "Medigap" group. Therefore, a limited number of retirees with insurance premiums fully paid by previous employers may be included in the Medicare Only group.

9. The insurance parameters in the regression model were highly significant, with values of 1.02 for 1980 and 0.98 for 1990, as shown in Table 6.6. Since the dependent variable is in logged form, health insurance coverage results in an increase of roughly 100 percent in expenditures on health goods and services excluding insurance premiums.

Chapter 7

Trends and the Future

Significant social and demographic shifts are occurring as a result of the tremendous growth in the elderly population (age 65+). This group expanded from 4 percent of the population at the turn of the century to 13 percent in 1996. By 2030 it is expected to increase to 20 percent. Furthermore, the greatest growth has occurred for the oldest old group (age 85+), which will represent 2.4 percent of the population in 2030.

Two remarkable changes in the characteristics of older Americans will continue to affect households, businesses, and national policies. First, the elderly are living longer and their life expectancies will continue to increase into the next century. From the turn of the century to 1993, male life expectancy at age 65 increased from 4 years to 15.3 years, and female life expectancy at age 65 increased from 7 years to 18.9 years. In 2050 a 65-year-old male's life expectancy will be 17.4 years and a female's at age 65 will be 22.4 years. Second, the labor force participation rates for males age 55 to 64 declined from 83 percent in 1970 to 67 percent in 1996. These two notable shifts indicate a significantly longer period of retirement, which must be financed. Unless working life expands, the elderly will spend 30 percent more years in retirement than only two decades ago. These retirement years are likely to be healthier than in previous generations, as a recent study found a 14.5 percent decline in the rate of older persons who are unable to care for themselves. In other words, not only is life expectancy increasing, but active life expectancy is increasing as well ("Study: Elderly Enjoying Longer, Healthier Lives," 1997). These unprecedented changes in the structure of the population will have significant impacts on all aspects life in the United States.

IMPACTS ON HOUSEHOLDS

The last 30 years have witnessed significant increases in the real disposable income of retirees, driven especially by the indexing of Social Security to inflation. Dependence on Social Security increased from 34 to 42 percent of income. As earnings have declined with reductions in labor-force participation from 29 to 18 percent of income, the elderly rely more on pension and asset income. These changes indicate greater recognition of retirement planning despite the fact that savings rates have decreased over time. Savings rates vary across retiree household types, as married couples continue to save while single households dissave. In particular, elderly single women dissave at unsustainable rates both immediately following retirement and on a continuing basis.

Because housing equity is one of the largest household assets in the United States, the savings rate is understated by the amount of equity payments made each year. Since a large share of retirees live in owner-occupied housing, their saving picture is not measured completely by financial assets. However, the use of housing equity as an effective asset is hampered by its relative illiquidity and the reluctance of the elderly to pursue reverse equity mortgages.

Although the elderly have generally been known as generous donors, their budget share and MPC for gifts and contributions declined over time for all household types. Their MPC for cash gifts and contributions fell more than for any other expenditure category. This decline has been attributed to tax changes that substantially lowered tax rates. Increased uncertainty about future health care expenses and longer life expectancies are also contributing factors. Interestingly, single females give more than either couples or single males. The largest drop in budget shares for giving occurred for the highest-income group (from 18 percent to 11 percent) and for the oldest old (from 10 percent to 4 percent). But the oldest old continued to donate substantially more over time than the younger old. Overall, nonprofit organizations need to consider our findings of declines in giving by the elderly so that they can adjust their strategies in line with these expenditure changes.

Our research identifies the shift toward leisure activities of the retired, which was not previously quantified in detail. Leisure desires are considerably higher for the retired than the nonretired, as shown by their greater MPCs for spending on entertainment, food away from home, other vehicle expenses, and public transportation. Upon entry into retirement, the MPC for our constructed category of trips increased dramatically (from 0.02 to 0.08), and the income elasticity for trips also increased sharply (from 0.42 to 1.11). This indicates that trips become a luxury good as persons move into retirement. Further, the desire for leisure doubled over time, as measured by the sum of the MPCs (0.14) for leisure activities.

As the MPC for leisure activities increased, the MPC for housing declined over time from 0.35 to 0.19. This sharply reduced propensity to spend on housing may be due to retirees travelling more or to their high percentage of homes owned without a mortgage. Housing is a particularly important commodity for single females, who spent larger amounts on housing than single males or married couples, and the differentials widened over time. This is closely related to the large percentage of elderly women living alone, a share that doubled from 26 percent to 52 percent in the past 30 years.

Elderly out-of-pocket health care expenditures increased 44 percent from 1980 to 1990 in real dollars, compared to 29 percent for the nonelderly. The budget share allocated to health care is largest for the low-income groups who do not receive financial assistance. The biggest change over time in health expenditures is in insurance, for which the elderly spent 106 percent more in 1990 than in 1980 (in real dollars). While they had a 4 percent decrease in spending for medical services, spending on drugs and medical supplies increased 52 percent, reflecting Medicare's lesser coverage of these items as well as increased utilization.

The proclivity of the elderly to purchase health care is closely tied to insurance coverage and age (and life expectancy). Interestingly, the importance of income declined (over the 1972–1987 period) as a determinant of the purchase of health care (including insurance costs). Health care has clearly become more of a necessity good over time, as measured by marked declines in income elasticity. Furthermore, income (in 1990) is not a significant explanatory variable for out-of-pocket health care expenditures (exclusive of insurance payments) for the high-income elderly. In other words, as incomes increase for high-income elderly households, their expenditures on health goods and services do not significantly increase, indicating adequate levels of health care at higher incomes. However, our findings indicate that medical expenses constitute a luxury for lower-income elderly households, despite the universality of Medicare for those age 65 and over.

Age became a more influential determinant of health care spending, as age elasticity increased for both medical services and health insurance. This indicates that the oldest old, faced with increased life expectancies, are more inclined to purchase health care, and more high-technology care is available.

The growing number of elderly presents challenges for many families in the near future. The "parent-support" ratio (the number of persons 85 years and older per 100 persons age 50 to 64 years) was 3 in 1950, 10 in 1993, and will rise to 29 by 2050, a tenfold increase over the course of a century. These challenges will require careful planning by all family members to adequately provide for elderly expenditures in the next century.

IMPACTS ON BUSINESS

As the elderly population grows, their discretionary purchasing power is fueling their ability to purchase the leisure goods and health care they desire. Cities and communities vie to attract retirees, with their discretionary spending, as visitors and residents. Many industries have only recently begun to recognize this substantial market power and to target older Americans as a significant consumer group. For example, the entertainment industry now caters to senior citizens with special attractions and venues. Growth of segments of the health care industry, including long-term care and home health care, are driven by the expanding elderly population. Medicare continues to be the largest funder of the hospital industry and the mainstay for funding graduate medical education. In addition, Medigap policies represent an increasing share of the market for health insurance.

An example of business's growing awareness of the considerable purchasing power of older households is seen in a recent analysis by a major retailer. Silver (1996) projects that consumers over age 55 will become the premier purchasing group in the 2000 to 2010 period. He predicts that not only will this group grow more rapidly than younger groups, but also this growth will be concentrated at higher levels of income. Those over age 55 with incomes in the $50,000 to $70,000 range are projected to increase three times as fast as the average population growth; and the annual growth rate for those over age 55 with incomes over $70,000 is projected to be four times the average. This provides an example of the potential market impact that today's baby boomers will have as they age.

Another example of business reacting to elderly consumers' special needs is the adaptations made by automobile manufacturers. Automakers have recognized that making driving easier for persons with physical limitations makes good business sense as the U.S. population ages. Nearly every automaker consults with the elderly and disabled in designing new vehicles. Given our findings of the high propensity of the elderly to travel, these redesigns will continue to strengthen the demands of the elderly for automotive travel in the future ("Automakers Making Driving Easier," 1997).

POLICY IMPLICATIONS

The unique challenges of an aging population pose serious policy issues for the United States. Entitlements that provide a safety net for the elderly are the dominant force determining federal budget deficits. The U.S. Council of Economic Advisors (1997) projects that without any policy changes, federal expenditures on Social Security, Medicare, and Medicaid would consume total government revenue by the year 2050.

Despite the general increases in elderly income and apparent living standards, the problems of low-income elderly, especially single women, will remain. Their major financial problem is affordable housing, which consumes a sizable share of their total budget. For those without family support, housing supplements are needed to promote their welfare. In contrast, many older households find their wealth tied up in housing. For this group additional policies to facilitate downsizing housing are needed. The 1997 federal tax changes will facilitate this downsizing by expanding the tax exemption for a housing sale from $125,000 to $500,000.

Financing health care for the elderly will become increasingly costly without major changes in either the structure of Medicare and Medicaid or stabilization of health care cost inflation. Although changes have been made to facilitate the use of Medicare HMOs, response by the elderly has been limited. Additionally, since these HMOs attract the more healthy elderly, they have not succeeded in reducing Medicare costs.

While health care cost inflation has declined for the past several years, there are indications that it will be difficult to contain these costs in the future. The number of elderly is growing, and the oldest old group is growing the fastest. Further, our results indicate that the oldest old have increased their demand for health care over time. Their increased out-of-pocket health expenditures for more insurance will make cost containment more difficult. They are not actively involved in the financial decisions when "purchasing" health care because their health insurance insulates them from the full marginal cost of these decisions.

The responses of households, businesses, and government to the dramatic changes in the elderly population and in their expenditure patterns are only beginning. We will need concerted and coordinated efforts at every level to cope successfully with the economic effects of our success in lengthening the life span. Continuing research is needed to provide empirical guidance for future adaptations to the growth of the elderly population.

Bibliography

Aaron, H. J. 1991. *Serious and unstable condition: Financing America's health care*. Washington, D.C.: The Brookings Institution.

Acs, Gregory, and John Sabelhaus. 1995. Trends in out-of-pocket spending on health care, 1980–92. *Monthly Labor Review*, 118(12): 35–45.

Allen, Jessie, and Alan Pifer. 1993. *Women on the front lines: Meeting the challenge of an aging America*. Washington, D.C.: The Urban Institute Press.

Ando, Albert, and Franco Modigliani. 1963. The Life Cycle Hypothesis of Saving: Aggregate implication and tests. *The American Economic Review*, 53(1): 55–84.

Arrow, Kenneth J. 1963. Uncertainty and the welfare economics of medical care. *The American Economic Review*, 53(5): 941–973.

Associated Press. 1996, December 3. Survey: Americans not saving enough for retirement dreams. Available at: http://cnn.com/US/9612/03/briefs/savings.ap/index.html

Associated Press. 1996, December 9. Poll: Most in U.S. expect less social security. Available at: http://cnn.com/US/9612/09/briefs/soc.sec.poll.ap/index.html.

Automakers making driving easier. 1997, March 26. *Dallas Morning News*, 2D.

Baker, Paul M. 1985. The status of age: Preliminary results. *Journal of Gerontology*, 40(4): 506–508.

Barnes, Robert, and Sheila Zedlewski. 1981. *The impact of inflation on the income and expenditures of elderly families*. Final report to the Administration on Aging. Washington, D.C.

Bennefield, Robert L. 1994. U.S. Bureau of the Census. *Health insurance, 1990 to 1992*, Table D (Current Population Reports, P70–37). Washington, D.C.: U.S. Government Printing Office.

Bernheim, B. Douglas. 1989. The timing of retirement: A comparison of expectations and realizations. In *The economics of aging,* ed. David A. Wise, 335–358. Chicago: University of Chicago Press.

Binstock, Robert H. 1991. Book reviews: In search of the poor elderly. *The Gerontologist*, 31(4): 563–565.

Boskin, Michael J., and Martin Feldstein. 1977. Effects of the charitable deduction on contributions by low-income and middle-income households: Evidence from the National Survey of Philanthropy. *Review of Economics and Statistics*, 59(3): 351–354.

Branch, E. R. 1987. Comparing medical care expenditures of two diverse U.S. data sources. *Monthly Labor Review*, 110(3): 15–18.

Brandt, Jeanette A. 1989. Housing and community preferences: Will they change in retirement? *Family Economics Review*, 2(2): 7–11.

Bridges, Benjamin, Jr., and Michael D. Packard. 1981. Price and income changes for the elderly. *Social Security Bulletin*, 44(1): 3–15.

Brown, Eleanor. 1987. Tax incentives and charitable giving: Evidence from new survey data. *Public Finance Quarterly*, 15(4): 386–396.

Burkhauser, Richard V. 1994. Protecting the most vulnerable: A proposal to improve Social Security insurance for older women. *The Gerontologist*, 34(2): 148–149.

Burkhauser, Richard V., G. J. Duncan, and R. Hauser. 1994. Sharing prosperity across the age distribution: A comparison of the United States and Germany in the 1980s. *The Gerontologist*, 34: 150–160.

Burkhauser, Richard V., and Timothy M. Smeeding. 1994. Social Security reform: A budget neutral approach to reducing older women's disproportionate risk of poverty. *Aging Studies Program Policy Brief, 2*. Syracuse, N.Y.: Syracuse University, Center for Policy Research.

Burkhauser, Richard V., and J. R. Wilkinson. 1983. The effect of retirement on income distribution: A comprehensive income approach. *The Review of Economics and Statistics*, 65: 653–658.

Burner, Sally T., Daniel R. Waldo, and David R. McKusick. 1992, Spring. National health expenditures projections through 2030. *Health Care Financing Review*, 14(1): 1–29.

Cafferata, Gail Lee. 1984. Private health insurance coverage and the Medicare population. *NCHSR national health care expenditures study* (Data Preview 18, U.S. Department of Health and Human Services Publication No. (PHS) 84–3362). Washington, D.C.: U.S. Government Printing Office.

Cafferata, Gail Lee. 1985. Private health insurance of the Medicare population and the Baucus legislation. *Medical Care*, 23(9): 1086–1096.

Canetto, Silvia Sara. 1992. Gender and suicide in the elderly. *Suicide and Life-Threatening Behavior*, 22(1): 80–97.

Chow, Gregory C. 1960. Tests of equality between subsets of coefficients in two linear regression models. *Econometrica*, 28(3): 591–605.

Chulis, George S., Franklin P. Eppig, Mary O. Hogan, Daniel R. Waldo, and Ross H. Arnett III. 1993, Spring. Health insurance and the elderly. *Health Affairs*, 12(1): 111–118.

Clark, Robert, Juanita Kreps, and Joseph Spengler. 1978. Economics of aging: A survey. *Journal of Economic Literature*, 16: 919–962.

Clark, Robert L., George L. Maddox, Ronald A. Schrimper, and Danuek A. Sumner. 1984. *Inflation and the economic well-being of the elderly*. Baltimore, Md.: Johns Hopkins University Press.

Clark, Robert L., and Danuek A. Sumner. 1985. Inflation and the real income of the elderly: Recent evidence and expectations for the future. *The Gerontologist*, 25(20): 146–152.

Clotfelter, Charles T. 1985. *Federal tax policy and charitable giving*. Chicago: University of Chicago Press.

Clotfelter, Charles T. 1989. *The impact of tax reform on charitable giving: A 1989 perspective*. The Office of Tax Policy Research, Working Paper Series, Working Paper No. 90–7. Ann Arbor: School of Business Administration, University of Michigan.

Crystal, Stephen, and Dennis Shea. 1990. The economic well-being of the elderly. *Review of Income and Wealth*, 36(3): 227–247.

Danziger, Sheldon, Jacques van der Gaag, Eugene Smolensky, and Michael K. Taussig. 1982–83. The Life-Cycle Hypothesis and the consumption behavior of the elderly. *Journal of Post-Keynesian Economics*, 5: 208–227.

Datan, Nancy. 1989. Aging women: The silent majority. *Women's Studies Quarterly*, 1 & 2: 12–18.

Davies, James B. 1981. Uncertain lifetime, consumption, and dissaving in retirement. *Journal of Political Economy*, 89(3): 561–577.

Davis, Karen, Gerald F. Anderson, Diane Rowland, and Earl P. Steinberg. 1990. *Health care cost containment*. Baltimore, Md.: Johns Hopkins University Press.

Daymont, T. N., and P. J. Andrisani. 1983. The health and economic status of very early retirees. *Aging and Work*, 6: 117–135.

Deaton, Angus. 1992. *Understanding consumption*. Oxford: Oxford University Press.

Diamond, Peter. 1992, November. Organizing the health insurance market. *Econometrica*, 60(6): 1233–1254.

Dornin, Rusty. 1996. Welfare reform squeezes grandparent caregivers. *CNN Interactive*, Dec. 8, 1996. Available: http://cnn.com/US/961208/grandparents.welfare/index.html.

Double-header: Older Americans see incomes rise, poverty fall. 1996, November. *AARP Bulletin*, 37(10): 3.

Elderly homeownership rate increases between 1980 and 1990. 1995. Census Bureau Reports. Available: http://blue.census.gov/Press-Release/cb95–25. (02/28/95).

Employee Benefit Research Institute. 1993. *Sources of health insurance and characteristics of the uninsured: Analysis of the March 1992 current population survey* (Special Report and Issue Brief No. 133). Washington D.C.: Employee Benefit Research Institute.

England, Paula, and George Farkas. 1986. Consumption, savings, and retirement. *Households, employment, and gender*, 103–118. New York: Aldine De Gruyter.

Espenshade, Thomas. J., and Rachel Eisenberg Braun. 1983. Economic aspects of an aging population and the material well-being of older persons. In *Aging in society: Selected reviews of recent research*, ed. Matilda White Riley, Beth B. Hess, and Kathleen Bond, 25–51. Hillsdale, N.J.: Lawrence Erlbaum.

Exter, Thomas. 1987. Incomes of the mature market. *American Demographics*, 9(12): 62.

Fahs, Marianne C. 1993. Preventive medical care: Targeting elderly women in an aging society. In *Women on the front lines: Meeting the challenge of an aging America,* ed. Jessie Allen and Alan Pifer, 105–132. Washington, D.C.: The Urban Institute Press.

Families USA Foundation. 1992, February. *The health cost squeeze on older Americans*. Washington, D.C.: Families USA Foundation.

Fareed, A. E., and G. D. Riggs. 1982. Old-young differences in consumer expenditure patterns. *The Journal of Consumer Affairs*, 16(1): 152–160.

Federman, Maya, Thesia I. Garner, Kathleen Short, W. Boman Cutter IV, John Kiely, David Levine, Duane McGough, and Marilyn McMillen. 1996. What does it mean to be poor in America? *Monthly Labor Review*, 119(5): 3–17.

Feldstein, Paul J. 1993. *Health care economics*. 4th ed. Albany: Delmar Publishers.

Ferraro, Kenneth F. 1990, January. Cohort analysis of retirement preparation, 1974–1981. *Journal of Gerontology: Social Sciences*, 45: S21–31.

Fethke, Carol C. 1989. Life-cycle models of savings and the effect of the timing of divorce on retirement economic well-being. *Journal of Gerontology: Social Sciences*, 44(3): S121–S128.

Foner, Anne, and Karen Schwab. 1983. Work and retirement in a changing society. In *Aging in society: Selected reviews of recent research*, ed. Matilda White Riley, Beth B. Hess, and Kathleen Bond, 71–93. Hillsdale, N.J.: Lawrence Erlbaum.

Foster, Susan E., and Jack A. Brizius. 1993. Caring too much? American women and the nation's caregiving crisis. In *Women on the front lines: Meeting the challenge of an aging America*, ed. Jessie Allen and Alan Pifer, 47–74. Washington, D.C.: The Urban Institute Press.

Frank, Robert H. 1985. *Choosing the right pond: Human behavior and the quest for status*. New York: Oxford University Press.

Friedman, Milton. 1957. *A theory of consumption function*. Princeton, N.J.: Princeton University Press.

van der Gaag, Jacques, and Eugene Smolensky. 1982, March. True household equivalence scales and characteristics of the poor in the United States. *Review of Income and Wealth.* 28(1): 277–308.

Garfinkel, Steven A., Arthur J. Bonito, and Kenneth R. McLeroy. 1987, Fall. Socioeconomic factors and Medicare supplemental health insurance. *Health Care Financing Review*, 9(1): 21–29.

Garfinkel, Steven A., Gerald F. Riley, and Vincent G. Iannacchione. 1988. High-cost users of medical care. *Health Care Financing Review*, 9(4): 41–52.

Garner, Thesia I. 1987. Income reporting in the U.S. consumer expenditure survey. *The Proceedings.* American Council on Consumer Interests 33rd Annual Conference, April 1987, Denver. Columbia, Mo.: American Council on Consumer Interests.

Gendell, M., and J. S. Siegel. 1992. Trends in retirement age by sex, 1950–2005. *Monthly Labor Review*, 115(7): 22–29.

Gieseman, Raymond. 1987. The Consumer Expenditure Survey: Quality control by comparative analysis. *Monthly Labor Review*, 110(3): 8–14.

Glasse, Lou. 1993. Housing crisis for older women. *Journal of Housing*, 50(4): 135–136.

Gollub, James, and Harold Javitz. 1989, June. Six ways to age. *American Demographics*, 11(6): 28–30, 35, 56–57.

Grad, Susan. 1990. Income change at retirement. *Social Security Bulletin*, 53(1): 210.

Grad, Susan. 1994. *Income of the population 55 or older, 1992.* U.S. Department of Health and Human Services Social Security Administration Office of Research and Statistics, 13–11871. Washington, D.C.: U.S. Government Printing Office.

Gramm, Phil. 1997, February 4. How to avoid Medicare's implosion. *The Wall Street Journal*, A18.

Greene, William H. 1990. *Econometric analysis.* New York: Macmillan.

Greene, William H. 1992. *LIMDEP user's manual and reference guide, Version 6.0.* Ballport, N.Y.: Econometric Software, Inc.

Harris, Richard J. 1986. Recent trends in the relative economic status of older adults. *Journal of Gerontology*, 41(3): 401–407.

Harrison, Beth. 1986. Spending patterns of older persons revealed in expenditure survey. *Monthly Labor Review*, 109(10): 15–18.

Hay, Robert P. 1996, November. New welfare law will hurt "vulnerable older people." *AARP Bulletin*, 37(10): 4.

Hayward, Mark D., and William R. Grady. 1990. Work and retirement among a cohort of older men in the United States, 1966–1983. *Demography*, 27(3): 337–356.

Health Care Financing Administration. 1997. *1996 statistics at a glance.* Washington, D.C. Available: http://www.hcfa.gov/stats/stathili.htm.

Hedstrom, Peter, and Ringen Stein. 1987. Age and income in contemporary society: A research note. *Journal of Social Policy*, 16(2): 227–239.

Henkel, William. 1989. Living well longer. *American Demographics*, 11(8): 24–25.

Herz, Diane E. 1995, April. Work after early retirement: An increasing trend among men. *Monthly Labor Review*. 118(4): 13–20.

Hildreth, G. J., and Eleanor Kelley. 1984–85. Family expenditures before and after retirement: A research model for measuring priorities. *International Journal of Aging and Human Development*, 20(2): 145–159.

Hitschler, Pamela B. 1993. Spending by older consumers: 1980 and 1990 compared. *Monthly Labor Review*, 116(5): 3–13.

Hogarth, Jeanne M. 1989. Saving and dissaving in retirement. *Family Economics Review*, 2(2): 13–17.

Holahan, Carole. 1981. Lifetime achievement patterns, retirement and life satisfaction of gifted aged women. *Journal of Gerontology*, 36(6): 741–749.

Honig, Marjorie, and Giora Hanoch. 1985. Partial retirement as a separate mode of retirement behavior. *The Journal of Human Resources*, 20(1): 21–46.

Hopkins, Bruce R. 1982. *Charitable giving and tax-exempt organizations: The impact of the 1981 tax act*. New York: John Wiley.

Hurd, Michael D. 1987. Savings of the elderly and desired bequests. *American Economic Review*, 77(3): 298–312.

Hurd, Michael D. 1989, May. The economic status of the elderly. *Science*, 244: 659–663.

Hurd, Michael D. 1990. Research on the elderly: Economic status, retirement, and consumption and saving. *Journal of Economic Literature*, 28: 565–637.

Hurd, Michael, and John B. Shoven. 1982. Real income and wealth of the elderly. *American Economic Review*, 72(2): 314–318.

Jacobs, Eva, Stephanie Shipp, and Gregory Brown. 1989. Families of working wives spending more on services and nondurables. *Monthly Labor Review*, 112(2): 15–23.

Jacobs, Ruth Harriet. 1993. Expanding social roles for older women. In *Women on the front lines: Meeting the challenge of an aging America*, ed. Jessie Allen and Alan Pifer, 191–220. Washington, D.C.: The Urban Institute Press.

Kaiser Family Foundation. 1995. *The Medicare program*. Washington, D.C.: Kaiser Family Foundation, 1–4.

Keith, Pat M., and Frederick O. Lorenz. 1989. Financial strain and health of unmarried older people. *The Gerontologist*, 29: 684–691.

Kennelly, Barbara. 1994, May/June. Retirement security of women: The Pension Reform Act of 1993. *Contingencies*, 52–53.

Ketkar, Suhas L., and Whewan Cho. 1982. Demographic factors and the pattern of household expenditures in the United States. *Atlantic Economic Journal*, 10: 16–27.

Kmenta, J. 1986. *Elements of econometrics*. 2nd ed. New York: Macmillan.

Koelln, Kenneth, Rose M. Rubin, and Marion Smith Picard. 1995. Vulnerable elderly households: Expenditures on necessities by older Americans. *Social Science Quarterly*, 76(3): 619–633.

Kolodinsky, Jane, and Robert W. Walsh. 1992. Prices, income, and the economic status of older single women: Implications for health care and housing policies. *Forum for Social Economics*, 22(1): 48–59.

Lamphere-Thorpe, Jo-Ann, and Robert J. Blendon. 1993. Years gained and opportunities lost: Women and healthcare in an aging America. In *Women on the front lines: Meeting the challenge of an aging America*, ed. Jessie Allen and Alan Pifer, 75–104. Washington, D.C.: The Urban Institute Press.

Lazer, William, and Eric H. Shaw. 1987. How older Americans spend their money. *American Demographics*, 9(9): 36–41.

Leon, Joel. 1985. A recursive model of economic well-being in retirement. *Journal of Gerontology*, 40(4): 494–505.

Levit, Katherine R., Mark S. Freeland, and Daniel R. Waldo. 1990. National health care spending trends: 1988. *Health Affairs*, 9(2): 171–184.

Levit, Katherine R., Helen C. Lazenby, Bradley R. Braden, Cathy A. Cowan, Patricia A. McDonnell, Lekha Sivarajan, Jean M. Stiller, Darleen K. Won, Carolyn S. Donham, Anna M. Long, and Madie W. Stewart. 1996. National health expenditures. *Health Care Financing Review*, 18(1): 175–214.

Levitan, S. A. 1990. *Programs in aid of the poor*. 6th ed. Baltimore, Md.: Johns Hopkins University Press.

Levy, Frank. 1987. *Dollars and dreams: The changing American income distribution*. New York: Norton.

Liviatan, Nissan. 1961. Errors in variables and Engel curve analysis. *Econometrica*, 29: 336–362.

Long, S.H., R. F. Settle, and C. R. Link. 1982. Who bears the burden of Medicare cost sharing? *Inquiry*, 19: 222–234.

Longino, Charles F., Jr. 1988, June. The comfortably retired and the pension elite. *American Demographics*, 10: 22–25.

Longino, Charles F., Jr., and William H. Crown. 1991. Older Americans: Rich or poor? *American Demographics*, 13(8): 48–52.

Lubben, J. E., P. G. Weiler, and I. Chi. 1989. Health practices of the elderly poor. *American Journal of Public Health*, 79(6): 731–734.

Lusky, Richard A. 1986. Anticipating the need of the U.S. aged in the 21st century: Dilemmas in epidemiology, gerontology, and public policy. *Social Science Medicine*, 23(12): 1217–1227.

Maddala, G. S. 1983. *Limited dependent and qualitative variables in econometrics*. New York: Cambridge University Press.

Magrabi, Frances M., Young Sook Chung, Sanghee Sohn Cha, and Se-Jeong Yang. 1991. *The economics of consumption*. New York: Praeger.

Malveaux, Julianne. 1993. Race, poverty, and women's aging. In *Women on the front lines: Meeting the challenge of an aging America*, ed. Jessie Allen and Alan Pifer, 167–190. Washington, D.C.: The Urban Institute Press.

Manning, Willard G., Joseph P. Newhouse, Naihua Duan, Emmett B. Keeler, Arleen Leibowitz, and M. Susan Marquis. 1987. Health insurance and the demand for medical care: Evidence from a randomized experiment. *American Economic Review*, 77(3): 251–277.

Margo, Robert A. 1991. *The labor force participation of older Americans in 1900: Further results*. NBER Working Paper Series on Historical Factors in Long Run Growth, Working Paper No. 27. Cambridge, Mass.: National Bureau of Economic Research.

McCall, Patricia, and Kenneth C. Land. 1994. Trends in white male adolescent, young-adult, and elderly suicide: Are there common underlying structural factors? *Social Science Research*, 23: 57–81.

McConnel, Charles, and Firooz Deljavan. 1983. Consumption patterns of the retired household. *Journal of Gerontology*, 38: 480–490.

Meyer, D. R., and S. Bartolomei-Hill. 1994. The adequacy of Supplemental Security income benefits for aged individuals and couples. *The Gerontologist*, 34: 161–172.

Miller, Michael A. 1985. Age-related reductions in workers' life insurance. *Monthly Labor Review*, 108(9): 29–34.

Minkler, Meredith, and Robyn Stone. 1985. The feminization of poverty and older women. *The Gerontologist*, 25(4): 351–357.

Mirer, Thad W. 1979. The wealth-age relation among the aged. *American Economic Review*, 69: 435–443.

Mirer, Thad W. 1980. The dissaving behavior of the retired aged. *Southern Economic Journal*, 46: 1197–1205.

Modigliani, Franco. 1966. The Life Cycle Hypothesis of saving, the demand for wealth and the supply of capital. *Social Research*, 33: 160–217.

Moehrle, Thomas. 1990. Expenditure patterns of the elderly: Workers and nonworkers. *Monthly Labor Review*, 113: 34–41.

Moen, Jon R. 1990. Fewer older men in the U.S. work force: Technological, behavioral, and legislative contributions to the decline. *Economic Review*, 75(6): 16–31.

Moon, Marilyn. 1989. The economic situation of older Americans: Emerging wealth and continuing hardship. *Annual Review of Gerontology and Geriatrics: Varieties of Aging*, ed. George L. Maddox and M. Powell Lawton, 8: 102–131.

Moon, Marilyn. 1991. Consumer issues and the elderly. *The Journal of Consumer Affairs*, 24(2): 235–244.

Morris, Robert, and Scott A. Bass. 1988. A new class in America: A revisionist view of retirement. *Social Policy*, 18(4): 38–43.

Morrisey, Michael A., Gail A. Jensen, and Stephen E. Henderlite. 1990. Employer-sponsored health insurance for retired Americans. *Health Affairs*, 9(1): 57–73.

National Center for Health Statistics. 1993, August 31. *Monthly Vital Statistics Report*, 42(2S), Table 7. Hyattsville, Md.: Public Health Service.

National Center for Health Statistics. 1994. *Health United States, 1993*, 42(2S), Table 72. Hyattsville, Md.: Public Health Service.

Newhouse, Joseph P. 1994, Spring. Patients at risk: Health reform and risk adjustment. *Health Affairs*, 13(1): 132–146.

Newhouse, Joseph P., Willard G. Manning, Carl N. Morris, Larry L. Orr, Naihua
Duan, Emmett B. Keeler, Arleen Leibowitz, Kent H. Marquis, M. Susan
Marquis, Charles E. Phelps, and Robert H. Brook. 1981. Some interim results from a controlled trial of cost sharing in health insurance. *New England Journal of Medicine*, 305: 1501–1507.

Nieswiadomy, Michael, and Rose M. Rubin. 1991. Changes in household economic status upon entry into retirement. Paper presented at the 66th Annual Conference of the Western Economic Association International,
Seattle, July 1, 1991.

Nieswiadomy, Michael, and Rose M. Rubin. 1995. Changes in expenditure patterns of retirees, 1972–1973 and 1986–1987. *Journal of Gerontology: Social Sciences*, 50B(5): S274–S290.

Omenn, G. S. 1990. Prevention and the elderly: Appropriate policies. *Health Affairs*, 9(2): 80–94.

Passero, William D. 1996. Spending patterns of families receiving public assistance. *Monthly Labor Review*, 119(4): 21–28.

Paulin, Geoffrey. 1990. Consumer expenditures on travel, 1980–87: Research
summaries. *Monthly Labor Review*, 113(6): 56–60.

Peracchi, Franco, and Finis Welch. 1994. Trends in labor force transitions of older
men and women. *Journal of Labor Economics*, 12(2): 210–242.

Petersen, M. D., and D. L. White, eds. 1989. *Health care of the elderly*. Newbury
Park, Calif.: Sage Publications.

Piacentini, Joseph S., and Timothy J. Cerino. 1990. *EBRI databook on employee
benefits*. EBRI-ERF Publication. Washington, D.C.: Employee Benefit Research Institute.

Prais, S. J., and H. S. Houthakker. 1955. *The analysis of family budgets*. Cambridge, Eng.: Cambridge University Press.

Rice, Thomas. 1987. An economic assessment of health care coverage for the elderly. *The Milbank Quarterly*, 65(4): 488–520.

Robb, A. L., and J. B. Burbidge. 1989. Consumption, income, and retirement.
Canadian Economics Association, 22(3): 522–542.

Ross, Christine M., Sheldon Danziger, and Eugene Smolensky. 1987. Interpret-
ing changes in the economic status of the elderly, 1949–1979. *Contemporary Policy Issues*, 5(2): 98–112.

Rubin, Jeffrey I., and Virginia Wilcox-Gök. 1991. Health insurance coverage among
disabled medicare enrollees. *Health Care Financing Review*, 12(4): 27–37.

Rubin, Rose M. 1997. The economic status of older women. In *The handbook
on women and aging*, ed. Jean M. Coyle. Westport, Conn.: Greenwood ,
75–92.

Rubin, Rose M., and Kenneth Koelln. 1993. Out-of-pocket health expenditure differentials between elderly and non-elderly households. *The Gerontologist*,
33(5), 595–602.

Rubin, Rose M., and Kenneth Koelln. 1996. Elderly and nonelderly expenditures on necessities in the 1980s. *Monthly Labor Review*, 119(9): 24–31.

Rubin, Rose M., Kenneth Koelln, and Roger K. Speas, Jr. 1995a. The impact of Medigap insurance on out-of-pocket health expenditures by older Americans over the 1980s. *Journal of Economics and Finance*, 19(2): 153–170.

Rubin, Rose M., Kenneth Koelln, and Roger K. Speas, Jr. 1995b. Out-of-pocket health expenditures by elderly households: Change over the 1980s. *Journal of Gerontology: Social Sciences*, 50B(5): S291–S300.

Rubin, Rose M., and Michael Nieswiadomy. 1992. Changes in expenditure patterns of the retired: 1972–73 and 1986–87. Paper presented at the 67th Annual Conference of the Western Economic Association International, San Francisco, July 10, 1992.

Rubin, Rose M., and Michael Nieswiadomy. 1994. Expenditure patterns of retired and non-retired persons. *Monthly Labor Review*, 117(4): 10–21.

Rubin, Rose M., and Michael Nieswiadomy. 1995. Economic adjustments of households on entry into retirement. *Journal of Applied Gerontology*, 14(4): 467–482.

Ruffin, M. D. 1989. Cutting back on consumption: The experience of older households. *Family Economics Review*, 2(3): 2–7.

Schneider, Edward L., and Jack M. Guralnik. 1990. The aging of America: Impact on health care costs. *Journal of the American Medical Association*, 263: 2335–2355.

Scholl, Kathleen K., and Marilyn Moon. 1988. *Dispelling the myth of the "undeserving rich"* (Report No. 8805). Washington, D.C.: The Public Policy Institute, Division of Legislation, Research and Public Policy, American Association of Retired Persons.

Schulz, James H. 1992. *The economics of aging.* 5th ed. New York: Auburn House.

Schulz, James H. 1995. *The economics of aging.* 6th ed. New York: Auburn House.

Schwenk, Frankie N. 1990a. A comparison of households headed by persons 55 to 65 years of age: Retired and employed. *Family Economics Review*, 3(3): 19–25.

Schwenk, Frankie N. 1990b. Households with expenditures for health insurance. *Family Economics Review*, 3(1): 2–6.

Schwenk, Frankie N. 1991. Women 65 years or older: A comparison of economic well-being by living arrangement. *Family Economics Review*, 4(3): 2–8.

Schwenk, Frankie N. 1993. Changes in the economic status of America's elderly population during the last 50 years. *Family Economics Review*, 6(1): 18–27.

Shapiro, Martin F., Rodney A. Hayward, Howard E. Freeman, Seymour Sudman, and Christopher R. Corey. 1989. Out-of-pocket payments and use of care for serious and minor symptoms. *Archives of Internal Medicine*, 149: 1645–1648.

Shapiro, Martin F., John E. Ware, and Cathy D. Sherbourne. 1986. Effects of cost sharing on seeking care for serious and minor symptoms: Results of a randomized controlled trial. *Annals of Internal Medicine*, 104: 246–251.

Silver, Ira. 1996, November 15. Discretionary spending power of the elderly. Speech by the chief economist of JC Penney to the Dallas Economists' Club, Dallas, Tex.

Silverman, Celia, Michael Anzick, Sarah Boyce, Sharyn Campbell, Ken McDonnell, Annmarie Reilly, and Sarah Snider. 1995. *EBRI databook on employee benefits*. 3rd edition. Washington, D.C.: Employee Benefit Research Institute.

Slesnick, Daniel T. 1992, November. Aggregate consumption and saving in the postwar United States. *Review of Economics and Statistics*, 74(4): 585–597.

Smeeding, Timothy M. 1989. *The economic well-being of the elderly—past, present, and future* (EBRI Issue Brief No. 96). Washington, D.C.: Employee Benefit Research Institute.

Smeeding, Timothy M., and Lavonne Straub. 1987. Health care financing among the elderly: Who really pays the bills? *Journal of Health Politics, Policy and Law*, 12: 35–52.

Smith, Richard J., and Richard W. Blundell. 1986. An exogeneity test for a simultaneous equation Tobit model with an application to labor supply. *Econometrica*, 54(3): 679–685.

Snyder, Donald C. 1989. A data base with income and assets of new retirees by race and Hispanic origin. *Review of Black Political Economy*, 17: 73–81.

Soberon-Ferrer, Horacio, and Rachel Dardis. 1991, March. Determinants of household expenditures for services. *Journal of Consumer Research*, 17: 385–397.

Social Security Administration. 1988, February. *Social Security Bulletin*, 51(2): Table 14.

Soldo, Beth J., and Emily M. Agree. 1988. America's elderly. *Population Bulletin*, 43(3). Washington, D.C.: Population Reference Bureau, 1–53.

Stoller, Eleanor P., and Michael A. Stoller. 1987. The propensity to save among the elderly. *The Gerontologist*, 27(3): 314–320.

Strate, John M., and Steven J. Dubnoff. 1986. How much income is enough? Measuring the income adequacy of retired persons using a survey based approach. *Journal of Gerontology*, 41(3): 393–400.

Study: Elderly enjoying longer, healthier lives. 1997. *CNN Interactive*, March 17, 1997. Available: http://cnn.com/Health/9703/17/elderly/health.ap/index.html.

Survey: Americans not saving enough for retirement dreams. 1996. *CNN Interactive*, Dec. 3, 1996. Available: http://cnn.com/US/961203/savings.ap/ index.html.

Taeuber, Cynthia M., and Jessie Allen. 1993. Women in our aging society: The demographic outlook. In *Women on the front lines: Meeting the challenge of an aging America,* ed. Jessie Allen and Alan Pifer, 11–46. Washington, D.C.: The Urban Institute Press.

Texas Institute for Research & Education on Aging. 1997, January. Consumers flunk long-term quiz. *Newsletter*, 6(1): 3.

Torrey, Barbara Boyle, and Cynthia M. Taeuber. 1986. The importance of asset income among the elderly. *Review of Income and Wealth*, 32(4): 443–449.

U.S. Bureau of the Census. 1981. *Statistical abstract of the United States: 1981.* 102d ed. Washington, D.C.: U.S. Government Printing Office.

U.S. Bureau of the Census. 1989. *Statistical abstract of the United States 1989.* 109th ed. Washington, D.C.: U.S. Government Printing Office.

U.S. Bureau of the Census. 1993. *Statistical abstract of the United States: 1993.* 113th ed. Washington, D.C.: U.S. Government Printing Office.

U.S. Bureau of the Census, 1994a. *Educational attainment in the United States: March 1992 and 1993* (Current Population Reports, P20–476). Washington, D.C.: U.S. Government Printing Office.

U.S. Bureau of the Census. 1994b. *Population projections of the United States by age, sex, race, and Hispanic origin: 1995–2050* (Current Population Reports, Series P25–1130). Washington, D.C.: U.S. Government Printing Office.

U. S. Bureau of the Census, 1994c. *Statistical abstract of the United States: 1994.* 114th ed. Washington, D.C.: U.S. Government Printing Office.

U.S. Bureau of the Census. 1995a. *Money income in the U.S., 1994* (Current Population Reports, Series P60–185). Washington, D.C.: U.S. Government Printing Office.

U.S. Bureau of the Census. 1995b. *Statistical abstract of the United States: 1995.* 115th ed. Washington, D.C.: U.S. Government Printing Office.

U.S. Bureau of the Census. 1996a. *Historical poverty tables—persons.* Table 3, Poverty status of persons, by age, race, and Hispanic origin. U.S. Bureau of the Census Web Site. Available: http://www.census.gov/hhes/poverty/histpov/hstpov3.html.

U.S. Bureau of the Census. 1996b, September. *Poverty in the United States: 1995* (Current Population Reports, P60–194). Washington D.C.: U.S. Government Printing Office.

U.S. Bureau of the Census. 1996c. *65+ in the United States* (Current Population Reports, Special Studies, P23–190). Washington, D.C.: U.S. Government Printing Office.

U.S. Bureau of the Census. 1996d. *Statistical abstract of the United States: 1996.* 116th ed. Washington, D.C.: U.S. Government Printing Office.

U.S. Bureau of the Census. 1997. *Resident population of the United States: Estimates by age and sex.* U.S. Bureau of the Census Web Site. Available: http://www.census.gov/population/estimates/nation/intfile2–1.txt

U.S. Council of Economic Advisors. 1988. *Economic report of the president.* Washington, D.C.: U.S. Government Printing Office.

U.S. Council of Economic Advisors. 1997. *Economic report of the president.* Washington, D.C.: U.S. Government Printing Office.

U.S. Department of Commerce. 1996, September 26. Weighted average poverty thresholds in 1995. U.S. Bureau of the Census, Washington D.C. Unpublished data.

U.S. Department of Health and Human Services. 1991. *Health insurance, use of health services, and health care expenditures*. National Medical Expenditure Survey. Research Findings 12. Washington D.C.: U.S. Department of Health and Human Services.

U.S. Department of Health and Human Services. 1994. *Fast facts & figures about Social Security*. Social Security Administration, Office of Research and Statistics. Washington D.C.: U.S. Department of Health and Human Services.

U.S. Department of Health and Human Services. 1996, June. *Income of the population 55 and over: 1994*. Social Security Administration. Washington, D.C.: U.S. Department of Health and Human Services.

U.S. Department of Labor, Bureau of Labor Statistics. 1974. *1972–1973 Consumer Expenditure Survey: Interview Survey detailed public use tape No.2 documentation*. Washington, D.C.: U.S. Government Printing Office.

U.S. Department of Labor, Bureau of Labor Statistics. 1981. *Comparison of 1972–73 and 1980–81 Surveys: Appendix C* (BLS Bulletin 2225). Washington, D.C.: U.S. Government Printing Office.

U.S. Department of Labor, Bureau of Labor Statistics. 1988. *1986 Consumer Expenditure Survey: Interview Survey detailed public use tape documentation*. Washington, D.C.: U.S. Government Printing Office.

U.S. Department of Labor, Bureau of Labor Statistics. 1989. *1987 Consumer Expenditure Survey: Interview Survey detailed public use tape documentation*. Washington, D.C.: U.S. Government Printing Office.

U. S. Department of Labor, Bureau of Labor Statistics. 1990a. *Consumer Expenditure Survey: Quarterly data from the Interview Survey* (Fourth Quarter 1989, Report 797). Washington, D.C.: U.S. Department of Labor.

U.S. Department of Labor, Bureau of Labor Statistics. 1990b. *1989 Consumer Expenditure Survey: Interview Survey detailed public use tape documentation*. Washington, D.C.: U.S. Department of Labor.

U.S. Department of Labor, Bureau of Labor Statistics. 1991a, November 22. *News* (USDL: 91–607). Washington, D.C.: U.S. Department of Labor.

U.S. Department of Labor, Bureau of Labor Statistics. 1991b. *1990 Consumer Expenditure Survey: Interview Survey detailed public use tape documentation*. Washington, D.C.: U.S. Department of Labor.

U.S. Department of Labor, Bureau of Labor Statistics. 1992, December. *Consumer expenditures in 1991* (Report 835). Washington, D.C.: U.S. Department of Labor.

U.S. Department of Labor, Bureau of Labor Statistics. 1996. *Consumer Expenditure Survey, 1995*, Table 3. Available at: gopher://hopi2.bls.gov:70/00/special%20requests/ce/standard/1995/age.prn.

U.S. Department of Labor, Bureau of Labor Statistics. 1997, January 30. Employee tenure in the mid-1990s. *News*. 1–4.

U.S. Senate Special Committee on Aging, the American Association of Retired Persons, the Federal Council on the Aging, and the U.S. Administration on

Aging. 1991. *Aging America: Trends and projections*. 1991 ed. Washington, D.C.: U.S. Department of Health and Human Services.

Von Weizsacker, Robert K. 1989. Demographic change and income distribution. *European Economic Review*, 33: 377–388.

Waldo, Daniel R., Sally T. Sommefeld, David R. McKusick, and Ross H. Arnett III. 1989. Health care financing trends: Health expenditures by age group, 1977 and 1987. *Health Care Financing Review*, 10(4): 111–120.

Walker, Retia Scott, and Frankie N. Schwenk. 1991. Income and expenditure patterns of consumer units with reference person age 70 to 79 and 80 or older. *Family Economics Review*, 4(1): 8–13.

Warlick, Jennifer L. 1985. Why is poverty after 65 a woman's problem? *Journal of Gerontology*, 40(6): 751–757.

A warning sign. 1996. *U.S. News & World Report*. October 21: 30.

Weaver, David A. 1994. The work and retirement decisions of older women: A literature review. *Social Security Bulletin*, 57(1): 3–24.

Wilcox, David W. 1991. Household spending and saving: Measurement, trends, and analysis. *Federal Reserve Bulletin*, 77(1): 1–17.

Wilcox-Gök, Virginia, and Jeffrey Rubin. 1992, September. Private health insurance and the utilization of medical care by the elderly. Working Paper No. 92–14. Department of Economics, Rutgers—The State University of New Jersey.

Wilensky, Gail R. 1982. Government and the financing of health care. *American Economic Review*, 72: 202–207.

Wolf, D. A., and B. J. Soldo. 1988. Household composition choices of older unmarried women. *Demography*, 25: 387–403.

Wu, Ke Bin. 1995, November. Recipiency of entitlement and other safety-net program benefits among families in 1993. *Data Digest*. Public Policy Institute, American Association of Retired Persons.

Zweifel, Peter. 1990. Aging: The great challenge to health care reform. *European Economic Review*, 34: 646–658.

Index

About the Authors

ROSE M. RUBIN is Professor of Economics at the University of Memphis. She is coauthor of *Working Wives and Dual-Earner Families* (Praeger, 1994).

MICHAEL L. NIESWIADOMY is Professor of Economics at the University of North Texas.